A Practical Approach to International Operations

Recent Titles from Quorum Books

A Practical Approach to International Operations

MICHAEL GENDRON

QUORUM BOOKS

NEW YORK • WESTPORT, CONNECTICUT • LONDON

Library of Congress Cataloging-in-Publication Data

Gendron, Michael.
  A practical approach to international operations / Michael
Gendron.
      p. cm.
  Includes index.
  ISBN 0-89930-252-1 (lib. bdg. : alk. paper)
  1. International business enterprises—Management. I. Title.
HD62.4.G45 1988
658'.049—dc19   88-6698

British Library Cataloguing in Publication Data is available.

Library of Congress Catalog Card Number: 88-6698
ISBN: 0-89930-252-1

First published in 1988 by Quorum Books

Greenwood Press, Inc.
88 Post Road West, Westport, Connecticut   06881

Printed in the United States of America

The paper used in this book complies with the
Permanent Paper Standard issued by the National
Information Standards Organization (Z39.48-1984).

10 9 8 7 6 5 4 3 2 1

CONTENTS

EXHIBITS

A Practical Approach to International Operations

CHAPTER 1

INTERNATIONAL OPERATIONS: A PORTFOLIO CONCEPT

During the past fifteen years, U.S. companies have realized that the U.S. market is reaching a saturation point. As a result, U.S. company expansion into international markets has accelerated. Many successful companies have properly managed their operations in the 2 billion plus population markets outside the United States, realizing substantial profits. Poorly managed companies have lost billions of dollars. The cause:

The international market is not simply an extension of U.S. business practice.

Legal, political, and social environments vary substantially from country to country. A venture into any of these markets requires a different approach to business control than in the United States. This chapter will highlight some keys—or a commonsense approach—to maintaining effective financial management in this environment. Issues to be discussed in this chapter include (1) simplified reporting, (2) the international portfolio concept, (3) understanding currency effects, and (4) simplified communication.

SIMPLIFIED REPORTING

International business segments are generally the sum of many small operations and may not be large U.S.-sized organizations. For example, if a corporation includes an international and a domestic operation, each with 100 million dollars of sales, the international operation may appear to be similar to the U.S. segment. Since both U.S. and international segments are of similar size, we might expect identical reporting. However, international operations may be in many markets rather than concentrated in large business units.

Additional resources may be available in the United States, due to the potentially larger scale of operations. A domestic organization may have a central computer area with a concentrated force of Electronic Data Processing (EDP) experts, a finance organization with a staff of analysts, and a marketing organization with a staff of analysts. Although the international group may have total sales of 100 million dollars, the international organization may operate in 25 different markets. Imagine the resources available in a 4 million dollar company! There will be no staff of computer programmers and no staff of financial analysts or accountants. The overhead to support such staffs would likely result in losses for the offshore operation.

A simple reporting system for an international operation must include only that which is essential to run a small business!

If information is not required to manage a 4 million dollar company, costs are added to insure compliance with a U.S. standard, but not necessarily to improve the local market operation. Additional reporting may be done, but the headquarters should understand that these additional controls may reduce offshore effectiveness.

Simple reporting could be limited to a local currency year-to-date trial balance, comparing actual to plan, and perhaps comparisons to the prior year. *A brief narrative discussing highlights of the monthly activity should also be required.* This limited financial report should provide the most significant information related to the goals or success of the offshore operations.

In addition to the limited financial reporting, key operating ratios may be essential to proper management of the operation. Exhibit 1.1 is an example of a key operating ratio statement.

Note that the first item in the statement is exchange rate. If performance is reviewed in U.S. dollars, significant currency fluctuations could result in misjudgments about performance unless currency fluctuations are considered. The remaining items in the operating ratio statement may vary among industries. Each business should carefully analyze management objectives and select the factors critical to monitoring their success.

Exhibit 1.1 reflects several items that may prove to be major investments in the international area:

1. *Manpower.* Generally manpower should be closely monitored. In many countries, existing social and legal restrictions require companies to maintain a stable work force. Stability can be accomplished through penalties or incentives. In either case, manpower may be a large "sunk cost," when employees are hired.

2. *Capital invested.* Capital investments in foreign markets may provide substantial tax benefits for companies. However, large capital outlays may also result in reduced flexibility in daily operations. All companies involved in international business should consider their investment a long-term one, but they must maintain effective control to reduce the risks. Fixed asset markets offshore may be much "thinner" than in the United States. Offshore capital investments may result in premature obsolescence and high losses upon disposition without careful planning.

3. *Cash balance.* Cash balance and a summary of exposures represent potential gains and losses that could occur during any currency revaluations. Rapid cash flow to U.S. dollar deposits for a U.S. company may result in minimum exposure and lowest risk. Cash balance should be closely monitored.

4. *Exposures.* This portion of the report will identify foreign currency exposures by type of currency. Exposures could be listed as $(+)$ or $(-)$. As the treasury projects currency movements, management can estimate gains and losses on exchange.

In order to effectively design operating ratio statements, management must thoroughly analyze its business objectives and define factors critical to success. Reports should be modified as management priorities are refined.

THE INTERNATIONAL PORTFOLIO

The international operations of many companies can be viewed as a business portfolio, with varying risks in each offshore market. As in all portfolios, four risk or cash flow classifications can be identified:

1. *Developing markets.* These operations have high growth potential and a high concentration of market share.

2. *Maturing markets.* These companies generate (not use) cash. Characteristics of this market include high market share with little potential for high growth. The market is developing at a more mature rate.

3. *Matured markets.* These markets represent both low market share and low potential growth for the company.

4. *Undefined potential.* These markets represent open opportunities for the organization. However, since they are not proven performers, the term *undefined* is applied.

Exhibit 1.1
Operating Ratio Statement

	CURRENT MONTH				YEAR TO DATE		
		%	FAV	(UNF)		%	FAV	(UNF)
	AMOUNT	SALES	AMOUNT	%	AMOUNT	SALES	AMOUNT	%

EXCHANGE RATE

(000'S U.S. DOLLARS)

SALES
GROSS PROFIT
OPERATING EXPENSE
ACCOUNTS RECEIVABLE
    D.S.O.
INVENTORY
    M.O.H.
MANPOWER
CAPITAL INVESTED
CASH BALANCE

EXPOSURES:

    FRANCS
    DEUTCHEMARKS

D.S.O. = days sales outstanding
M.O.H. = month's (inventory) on hand

These classifications have been used by various consulting groups to better understand product or business portfolios as well as improve company resource allocation. Identical principles apply to the operations maintained in the international portfolio.

Segments of the business portfolio require specific skills, depending on the market's strategic classification. Business portfolio characteristics of each classification in the international operation could include "undefined" countries, "developing" countries, and "maturing" and "matured" countries.

Undefined countries require an entrepreneurial spirit. Personnel should be accustomed to developing business in unusual environments. Undefined countries may be identified in Latin America, Africa, and the Middle East. Individuals who have specialized by region (including language and customs) are generally the most successful. Company management should be prepared to deal with limited or reduced reporting as well as potentially high expenses for these developing markets. Business activity will not occur on a routine or continuous basis. Generally these areas require constant attention, and result in large, infrequent orders, due to restrictive import and licensing and banking regulations (obtaining letters of credit, sight drafts, etc., can be both time-consuming and expensive).

Management controls should be established with these operating characteristics in mind. For example, if sales occur only at the end of the month, a daily sales report would have little value.

Developing countries may have developed from undefined countries through distributor organizations or perhaps through acquisition. Although improved financial controls can be implemented in such developing countries, management must be prepared for major marketing and selling expenses. Controls for developing countries should be the minimum required to provide complete product line inventories and timely service to consumers. Although detailed reviews may not be appropriate for these companies, key operating ratios and performance versus plan should be closely monitored.

Maturing and matured countries require an exposure management review, rather than a detailed operations review. These countries generate cash and exposures, and should receive closer scrutiny by treasury services. Operations should be monitored through complete monthly reporting, but emphasis must be placed on exposure management. Cash in the international business segment can generate substantial losses simply through ownership.

UNDERSTANDING CURRENCY EFFECTS

It is all too easy to interpret an international operation/U.S. dollar financial statement (translated in accordance with FASB 52) as we would

for a U.S. corporation. However, in foreign operations, revaluing currencies may significantly impact sales, cost of sales, and expenses.

FASB 52 introduces new foreign operation's measurement criteria and
concepts. While a thorough review of the statement would be inappropri-
ate, information to better understand FASB 52 can be obtained from a
CPA. Chapter 3 includes additional highlights of the statement for reference. For example, if a Canadian operation were budgeted to have 10
million dollars (Canadian) of sales and 1 million dollars (Canadian) of
operating earnings, considering a $.95 Canadian dollar, how would a
$.10 devaluation affect performance (see Exhibit 1.2)?

Note that a $.10 devaluation affects operating earnings at the same
ratio as the operating earnings percent to sales in local currency. If
offshore responsibility were to realize operating earnings of $950,000
(U.S.), has the operation reached its objective? This example was prepared assuming the Canadian dollar was the functional currency (see
FASB 52 for more information).

If the U.S. dollar were the functional currency (refer to FASB 52 for a
complete description of how to determine the functional currency), sales
and operating earnings results would be adversely affected as shown in
Exhibit 1.3.

If the functional currency is considered the local currency, the gains or
losses due to changing currency values are recorded immediately in stockholders' equity rather than current year earnings. If the functional
currency is other than the country's local currency, current year earnings
will be affected by currency fluctuation.

In addition to operating P&L (profit and loss) exposures, balance sheet
exposures must be closely monitored. As stated earlier, cash ownership
can result in an exposure.

Exhibit 1.2
Example: Translation Impact

(000's omitted)

Funct Currency = Canadian $	Canadian $	U.S. $ @.95	U.S. $ @.85	Fav (Unf)
Sales	10,000	9,500	8,500	(1,000)
Cost	5,000	4,750	4,250	(500)
Gross Profit	5,000	4,750	4,250	(500)
Operating Expense	4,000	3,800	3,400	(400)
Profit Before Tax	1,000	950	850	(100)

Exhibit 1.3
Translation Impact on Profits

(000's)

	Canadian $	U.S. $ @ Actual @.95	U.S. $ @ Budget @.85
Sales	10,000	9,500	8,500
Cost of Sales	5,000	4,750	4,250
Gross Profit	5,000	4,750	4,250
Operating Expenses	4,000	3,800	3,400
Profit Before Tax	1,000	950	850

If, as in Exhibit 1.3, a $.10 devaluation of the Canadian dollar occurs, what is the value of currency?

Canadian	U.S. @ $.95	U.S. @ $.85
$1,000,000	$950,000	$850,000

Similar losses (or gains) can occur for uncollected (unpaid) "cash" equivalents, such as accounts receivable or accounts payable. Equity invested in operations can quickly disappear through currency movements.

Balance sheets can contain exposures never considered in a U.S. company. Consider that each account in the balance sheet is subject to the foreign exchange fluctuations of the foreign exchange market. Exhibit 1.4 reflects alternative valuations of the local currency balance sheet considering foreign exchange valuations. Note the impact on accounts generally considered to be low risk, or current assets. Cash, investments, accounts receivable, and inventories may generally be considered safe assets, but in the international operation ownership of these assets could be extremely risky. Liabilities in the international operation could present similar risks.

SIMPLIFIED COMMUNICATION

It may be difficult to understand how a 100 million dollar operation can be a "small business." Such an international operation could consist of 25 separate units, with sales of 4 million dollars each. If this concept is fact, it may be impossible to effectively administer without clear reporting channels.

Exhibit 1.4
Translation Impact: Balance Sheet

Description	Local Currency	U.S. @ .8	U.S. @ 1.0	U.S. @ 1.3
Cash	1,000	$800	$1,000	$1,300
Accounts Receivable	25,000	20,000	25,000	32,500
Inventory	40,000	32,000	40,000	52,000
Fixed Assets	30,000	24,000	30,000	39,000
Other Assets	5,000	4,000	5,000	6,500
Total Assets	101,000	80,800	101,000	131,300
Accounts Payable	5,000	4,000	5,000	6,500
Accruals	3,000	2,400	3,000	3,900
Long Term Debt	45,000	36,000	45,000	58,500
Total Liabilities	53,000	42,400	53,000	68,900
Net Assets	48,000	$38,400	$48,000	$62,400

As discussed earlier, large multinational corporations may have extensive staff to deal with daily operations. Specialists in EDP, treasury, finance personnel, and so on, can answer questions and also ask questions of offshore personnel. Since corporations may consist of numerous divisions, many specialists may request information from the offshore companies, resulting in duplication of effort. Exhibit 1.5 demonstrates the confusing communications that may actually be required to operate offshore subsidiaries.

A possible solution is to establish a team of international specialists who understand subsidiary operations. Information could be channeled through these specialists to reduce the communications overload. Exhibit 1.5 also demonstrates simplified communication.

Although specialists may not be the answer, U.S. management must be aware of the critical need for simplified communication. If the offshore operation is satisfying the "corporate" requirement," will the offshore personnel have sufficient resources with which to satisfy customer needs? The communication channels can be determined by performing a communications review. Each point of contact with the offshore units should be charted to determine frequency, content, and purpose. After charting has been completed, management must review the communication flow to determine if the best communication channels are being used to achieve the required results.

Exhibit 1.5
Simplified Communication

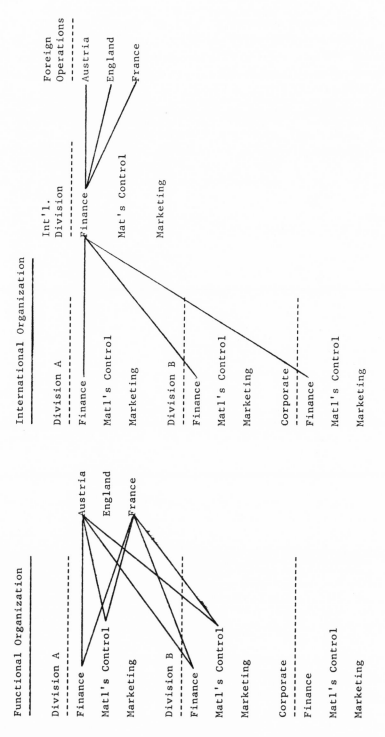

Functional Organization

International Organization

The objective of the review is to minimize the number of contacts with headquarters while achieving necessary control over the offshore operation. Chapter 4 includes more discussion about these communication channels.

SUMMARY

International operations represent an opportunity for increased business. However, basic common sense must be used in this area. It cannot be administered in the same way as U.S. operations. Legal, social, and economic environments are substantially different from those in the United States.

International operations require a flexible management style which adapts to unusual business conditions. In international operations, to simplify is to succeed.

CHAPTER 2

DECISION PYRAMID: A CONCEPTUAL REVIEW OF INTERNATIONAL OPERATIONS

Effective business management is complicated by two major factors: management experience and business environment.

Management experience. It is important to recognize that each manager's business experience and training is unique. There may be business managers with technical training (e.g., engineering) who have other business responsibilities (e.g., product marketing). Effective management will help personnel develop to their career potential. Management can be developed by identifying specific business responsibilities for each management position, and requiring periodic reporting. Periodic reporting will reinforce position requirements, and if properly defined, will develop the manager into an expert in that position.

Business environment. All multinational units operate in differing legal, political, and economic environments, and may sell different products (consumer goods, capital goods, chemicals, etc.). Multinational operations must adapt to continuously changing environments, but must also maintain control over their operation.

An effective reporting system will isolate the major environmental changes that affect a business, and raise decision responsibility to an appropriate level.

In order to simplify a multinational business and focus attention on specific management objectives, a well-designed communication system is essential. This communication system must provide meaningful, timely information that will raise decision responsibility to a proper level of authority. This chapter will discuss the "decision pyramid" concept of management and the communication system that allows it to work.

MANAGEMENT RESPONSIBILITIES

The "decision pyramid" is a three-dimensional figure designed to illustrate effective management reporting. As demonstrated in Exhibit 2.1, the various levels of the pyramid represent distinct levels of authority, responsibility, and management experience. Each level must have clearly defined objectives that contribute to corporate goals. As with normal management structure, each higher level has broader responsibilities and fewer participants.

Effective management will ensure that authority, responsibility, and necessary business experience are consistent within the organization. For example, an effective sales organization will assign responsibility for customer sales to a salesperson, while pricing and credit limits will be defined by management.

An effective organization will provide adequate training to personnel. Performance goals will be mutually established by employees and management. Performance reports will identify progress toward established

Exhibit 2.1
The Decision Pyramid

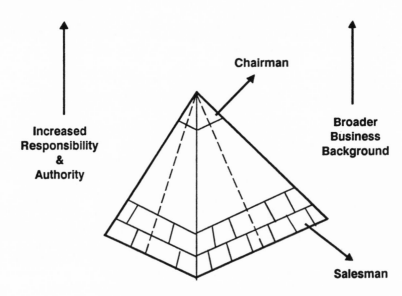

Side 1 = Authority
Side 2 = Responsibility
Side 3 = Business Experience

sales goals. If an employee exceeds his authority, the organization is not functioning effectively. For example, if a sales representative sells a product at a substantial unauthorized discount, control reports to management should identify the breach of authority before major costs are incurred. An effective business communication system will isolate and report any exception to the proper authority.

The development and design of such a communication system requires the following:

1. *Corporate objectives must be clearly defined.* All employees must be able to properly interpret them and understand their responsibilities.
2. *Management must provide a clear definition of subordinate responsibilities and authority.* Quantitative measures must be identified in the planning process so that each employee clearly understands his responsibilities and the limits of his authority.
3. *Management must define the specific accounting information that will be used for performance measurement.*

Each subordinate level within the organization is responsible for a narrower field of expertise and has less overall responsibility. Examples would include an accounting manager, whose responsibilities are limited to a specific technical discipline, or perhaps a regional general manager, whose responsibilities may be limited to the European region. A "general" manager must effectively translate corporate goals for these specialized managers, and ensure that goals are properly communicated to all company employees.

Exhibit 2.1 is an example of a decision pyramid. As we move from the base of the pyramid to its peak, the number of employees and management participants decrease. Note that the type of reporting changes as well.

The salesperson will receive reports that relate to his primary responsibility: customer sales. Progressing through the pyramid, note that the details become more summarized. Eventually, some of the details disappear, since upper management relies on subordinates' judgment.

DEFINITION OF CORPORATE OBJECTIVES

General management must translate corporate objectives into practical goals for each employee. The manager must understand the corporation's primary objectives so that tasks can be allocated to subordinates to satisfy those objectives. If a manager has effectively allocated department responsibilities, the department will satisfy the corporate objectives. The subordinate must understand his responsibilities, and also have the authority to control the factors ensuring task completion.

For example, if the corporate objective is a minimum annual earnings per share growth of 15 percent, certain actions are required.

1. *Statement of objectives.* The policy statement provides a clear definition of the chairman's interpretation of the stockholders' objectives: annual company earnings per share growth of 15 percent. The chairman may also define additional company responsibilities, such as a minimum return on sales of 25 percent.

2. *Interpretation.* The chairman may translate this objective to: (a) *Growth* in Division A of 20 percent earnings; growth in Division B of 15 percent earnings. (b) *Return on sales* in Division A of 25 percent operating earnings as a percent of sales, Division B of 35 percent operating earnings as a percent of sales.

3. *Action.* Division president A may translate these objectives to division management as: (a) *Sales growth* in the international segment of the division of more than 40 percent over the previous year; domestic sales must grow by more than 15 percent to achieve the 20 percent growth. (b) *Return on sales* in the international unit of 20 percent operating earnings as a percent of sales; domestic must maintain a 40 percent operating earnings return on sales, to achieve the 25 percent earnings growth.

These are better demonstrated in Exhibit 2.2. Note that goals must be developed for each strata of the pyramid to ensure that overall corporate goals are achieved.

It should be noted that each "translation" point may modify the management objective to ensure that subordinates can identify the objective within their level of responsibility and authority. Senior management must establish the relationship between the corporate goal and the subordinate goal.

For example, a sales manager may find it difficult to interpret a 40 percent operating earnings return on sales, but should understand achievement of an average realized selling price for a specific product's sales. The "translation" must have a supporting financial analysis that establishes the relationship of the corporate objective and the employee responsibility (e.g., 10 percent return on sales).

Appropriate control reports for general management would include:

Profit and loss statement

Balance sheet

Statement of cash flow

Variance analysis that isolates major deviations from corporate (division) goals

The control reports must highlight subordinate managers' responsibilities and current performance.

A brief management narrative supporting major variances from objectives should be included in a periodic progress report. Narratives should include an executive summary to highlight overall progress, and should

Exhibit 2.2
The Decision Pyramid

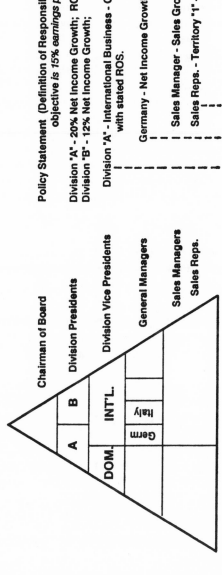

Chairman of Board — Policy Statement (Definition of Responsibilities) - Long-term Company objective is *15% earnings per share growth per year*. (1)

Division Presidents
Division "A" - 20% Net Income Growth; ROS Weighted Average
Division "B" - 12% Net Income Growth; 15% (2)

Division Vice Presidents
Division "A" - International Business - Growth 25% in Net Income (3) with stated ROS.

General Managers
Germany - Net Income Growth 20%, with ROS.

Sales Managers
Sales Manager - Sales Growth by Minimum 20%.

Sales Reps.
Sales Reps. - Territory "1" - Sales Growth 25%.

discuss business factors rather than just verbalizing the numbers in the schedule. For example, a progress report about a new product introduction could be included in the highlights. This could focus on the number of new customers, leads identified, advertisements placed, and so on. Long, detailed narratives may indicate that subordinates do not understand their authority and responsibility.

ASSIGNMENT OF SUBORDINATE RESPONSIBILITY

Subordinate responsibilities may be limited in a narrow or overall sense. A general manager must review corporate objectives, and translate these objectives to specific disciplines. Through evaluation of each subordinate's skills, the general manager must allocate available resources and assign responsibility to achieve the corporate goal.

Specific quantitative and measurable objectives as well as periodic reports must be established for each type of responsibility. Periodic reports should inform senior management of progress toward defined objectives. The reports must highlight the quantitative and measurable objectives assigned to subordinates.

For example, the general manager may review the corporate objective in relation to sales department resources. Translation of the corporate objective may result in the following quantifiable business objectives or responsibilities for the sales manager:

Minimum *unit productivity* of 20 percent over prior year

Minimum *gross profit rate* of 40 percent

Maximum overall *day sales outstanding* for the region of 60 days.

An appropriate control report for the sales manager would include the accounting information shown in Exhibit 2.3.

These reports concentrate the sales manager's attention on the primary corporate objectives. Brief comments supporting major variations from established objectives should accompany the periodic statement to the general manager.

Since the above objectives represent the sales department objectives, the sales manager must allocate his "salesman" resources to achieve the overall objectives. Similar reports for each customer should be available for each salesman so that he can monitor his progress toward obtaining objectives. As we proceed down through the management hierarchy, reports will include more detail to support the more specific objectives. Note in Exhibit 2.4 that each successive lower level on the decision pyramid includes more detail, due to the reduced level of responsibility.

Exhibit 2.3
Sales Manager Report

		Sales	Current	Month
Sales Representative	A/R Balance	Amount	F(U) to F/C	F(U) to P.Y.
Atlas Co.	$64,000	$7,000	$1,000	$1,000
Banner Smith Co.	127,000	26,400	6,000	0
:				
:				
:				
Total	$747,000	$290,000	$29,000	$58,000

Regional Manager

Territory A	$747,000	$290,000	$29,000	$58,000
Territory B	125,000	20,000	6,000	12,500
Territory C				
:				
:				
:				
Total	$3,400,000	$1,100,000	$65,000	$125,000

DEFINITION OF ACCOUNTING INFORMATION

Effective management will ensure that objectives are clearly defined and that periodic progress reports are prepared. These internal reports *must be prepared using existing accounting information.* The accounting department and general manager must plan the communication system. Measurement objectives and key operating ratios must be developed to report against company objectives. After management has "translated" corporate objectives and developed overall reports and key operating ratios, the accounting department must define components of the basic accounting transaction to satisfy the reporting requirement.

Accounting definitions should reflect the possibility of changing objectives and should be prepared as general guidelines to ensure that minor changes in objectives do not require a complete revision of the accounting

Exhibit 2.4
Example: Sales Hierarchy

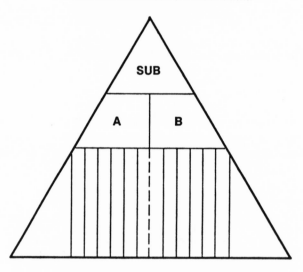

Region Activity:
20% Increase in Units

Territory A = **30% Increase**
Territory B = **15% Increase**

Customer Allocation....................

system. For example, region objectives could include unit productivity of 20 percent over the prior year. The general manager may "translate" this objective as follows:

A customer list must be prepared for territory A (e.g., Latin America) and territory B (e.g., the Far East) to properly measure unit productivity growth. An example of an ineffective method of defining territories A and B would be to prepare a list of existing customers and then to assign a territory code to each customer. This does not consider potential future territory reorganizations or new customer additions.

Preplanning future reporting needs would anticipate new customers. Preplanning would result in:

1. Definition of an accounting rule
2. Assigning existing customers to a territory using this rule

3. Assigning new customers to a territory based on the accounting rule defined.

Definition of a sales territory accounting rule in international operations may be accomplished by consulting a world atlas listing all countries/territories. Working closely with the marketing/sales department, general guidelines for territory definitions could include the following:

Prefix	Description
10	Latin America: All countries south of the United States, including Central America, South America, and the Caribbean region
20	Far East: All countries on the Asian continent, and countries in the Pacific basin
30	Europe: . . .
40	Africa: . . .

Assignment of customers to the territory can be completed by analyzing the marketing department needs. If, for example, there are separate distribution channels (e.g., distributors, OEMs or original equipment manufacturers, nonprofit organizations) accounting information should be encoded in customer I.D. numbers. For example:

I.D. #	Customer Name	Characteristics
10-4-300	Dan Smith Co.	Latin America Distributor
10-4-307	Riva Products	Latin America Distributor
20-2-475	Foo Lon Enterprise	Far East OEM
30-1-227	List Bus Co.	European nonprofit

As new customers are gained through expanded sales efforts, the accounting rule can be applied.

Effective preplanning may result in territory definition by geographic region. Since a simple accounting statistic has been defined, reporting against territory objectives can be done by sorting and summarizing the specific accounting data defined in the planning process. Reporting against objectives will be much simpler after the components of the basic accounting transactions have been defined. Well-developed accounting rules will result in an information matrix that can be used by management to more effectively allocate resources. Exhibit 2.5 shows an example matrix.

Exhibit 2.5
Sales Information Matrix

Sales	Distrib Channel				Product Line				
	O.E.M.	Dis'tor Retail	Non-Profit	Total	Shoes	Skirts	Shorts	Socks	Total

Region

Latin America

    Peru
    Colombia
    Bolivia
    ..
    ..
    ..

    Total

Far East

    Taiwan
    Korea
    Australia
    Singapore
    ..
    ..
    ..

    Total

SUMMARY

Preplanning and periodic reporting against clearly defined objectives will ensure an effective management structure. Several activities must occur before effective reporting can be accomplished:

1. Translation of corporate objectives to all levels of management
2. Clear definition of responsibility and authority
3. Clear definition of report objectives
4. Clear definition of accounting requirements

CHAPTER 3

UNDERSTANDING CURRENCY EFFECTS

International operations' financial statements can be reviewed in several different ways: from the simplest—that is, review the total of all international results as a single operation in U.S. dollars—and in a complicated way—that is, review each market separately, with full financial statements in both local currency and U.S. dollars. This chapter will discuss basic accounting regulations relating to translation of a foreign operation's financial statements, some alternative financial presentations, and a methodology with which to identify the appropriate level of reporting for an international operation.

During the past fifteen years, many international operations have suffered through alternate periods of success and failure partially due to extreme currency fluctuations. Certain companies with exceptionally skilled international managers have prospered during these periods. In this chapter, we will review:

1. The financial standards established by the Financial Accounting Standards Board (FASB) relating to foreign currency translation
2. Examples of currency translation effects in the income statement and balance sheet
3. A methodology for defining the management reporting content and frequency
4. A review of example reporting formats, focusing on P&L responsibilities

At the conclusion of the chapter, the reader should bettter understand international financial operations, and also some of the unusual management challenges in international oeprations.

International operations are significantly different from U.S.
operations.

HISTORY OF REPORTING

Until 1975, companies reported earnings using their best judgment and
broad guidelines established by the Accounting Principles Board (APB).
Currency fluctuations generally were not significant, due to the close
relationships of worldwide currencies. Management was less strictly gov-
erned by an accounting regulatory group, when compared to the 1980s.

In 1975 the Financial Accounting Standards Board implemented its
most restrictive policy relating to foreign currency translation (FASB 8).
As a result of FASB 8, certain currency fluctuations were required to be
recorded in the current year operating results. From 1975 to 1981, net
earnings and earnings per share were seriously affected by the rules established in FASB 8. The basis of FASB 8 seemed to be arbitrary, since results
of operations were not necessarily reflected in financial statements.
During that period, international management was unable to effectively
manage or predict the profitability of their international operations with
any assured results. Management reasoned that significant unpredictable
currency fluctuations should not represent an organization's earning
power, and should therefore not be considered in the current year's
performance.

The Accounting Standards Board considered the management critique
of FASB 8 and accepted the reasoning that current earnings should not be
affected by currency market volatility. In December 1981 the FASB
established a new standard relating to the translation of foreign currency
financial statements. The statement—FASB 52—has generally been considered to be a better representation of economic value in periods of
extreme currency fluctuations.

FASB 52—THE THEORY

FASB 52 has identified three basic concepts to use as the basis for the
translation or interpretation of a foreign operation's results: (1) functional
currency; (2) remeasurement of foreign currency operations; and (3) translation of foreign currency.

Functional Currency

Functional currency is a concept developed by the Accounting Standards Board which recognizes that foreign operations will generate busi-

ness and cash flows in many different currencies. Each successful business must be responsive to a world economy while subject to its unique economic environment. Although an operation may be responsive to many economic factors, there will be one primary economic environment that is the basis for management decisions.

For example, if a German subsidiary of a U.S. corporation incurs all manufacturing material costs and the majority of selling general and administrative costs (SG&A) in U.S. dollars, and the company has world-wide sales denominated in U.S. dollars, the primary environment affecting that operation is the U.S. dollar environment, even though the plant is in Germany. The dominant currency, or currency that the business is managed by, is the U.S. dollar. In this case, the functional currency is the U.S. dollar. Cash flows will also probably be measured in U.S. dollars, because that is the sales currency and the primary "added value" currency.

Operating Characteristics. Certain business operating characteristics can be used to determine if a different functional currency designation is required:

1. Billings should be reviewed to determine if sales are predominantly in a currency other than the local currency. If concentrated in another foreign currency, a functional currency designation should be considered to properly remeasure financial statements.
2. Product costs should be reviewed to identify any concentration in a specific currency other than the local currency. Another functional currency should be considered if costs are heavily dependent on a foreign currency.
3. A foreign operation heavily financed in another foreign currency may require a determination of another functional currency.

These considerations represent the management decision process. If decisions are generally made based on another foreign currency value, a functional currency should be used. The foreign operation should be carefully reviewed to determine if any of the above criteria have been met. If a functional currency is required, remeasurement gains and losses will result from currency fluctuations.

Remeasurement gains/losses are recognized in current operating results, because operating decisions are based on foreign currency relationships (e.g., selling prices may be adjusted, based on the relationship of currencies). Such decisions are current or short-term decisions compared to strategic decisions such as investment in a building. The remeasurement process will be discussed later.

The board has determined that currency variances should only affect monetary assets or items with immediate liquidating value. All other items (inventory, fixed assets, long-term financing, etc.) are not necessarily affected by short-term currency fluctuations. However, short-term fluctuations may affect the long-term investment value of the foreign operation. As such, company equity should be adjusted to reflect the changing value of these nonmonetary assets, but not through current earnings. The actual translation procedures will be illustrated later in this chapter.

Inflation. Historically, a country's inflation variance compared to a specific world currency (e.g., the U.S. dollar) would determine long-term or permanent valuation adjustment of a currency. In this instance, the board has been somewhat arbitrary and states that excessive inflation—or hyperinflation—should determine or be considered in the determination of reported results. The board has established that cumulative 3-year inflation of 100 percent requires that the U.S. dollar be used as the functional currency.

Remeasurement. If a functional currency other than the local currency has been defined, a "remeasurement" of the financial statements is required. Remeasurement is a term that describes the bridge between a functional currency and the translated financial statements. Remeasurement will convert financial statements from a functional currency (e.g., U.S. dollars) to the same local currency of the foreign subsidiary.

FASB—THE PROCEDURES

Two steps are required for proper translation and presentation of foreign financial statements: remeasurement and translation.

Remeasurement

The first step in preparing foreign financial statements requires that a functional currency be defined. If the functional currency is not the local currency, the financial statements must be remeasured to local currency prior to translation to U.S. dollars. Recall that the company "operating characteristics," or the cumulative inflation rate may require that a functional currency other than the local currency of the foreign subsidiary be defined and used.

The remeasurement process requires that certain accounts be translated at historical translation rates, that is, *the translation rates in effect when the original transaction occurred.* In general, the following accounts should be translated at historical rates:

—Marketable securities carried at cost (i.e., equity securities or debt securities not expected to be held until their maturity)

—Inventories carried at cost

—Prepaid expenses

—Fixed assets and related depreciation

—Patents, trademark licenses, and formulas

—Goodwill and other intangibles

—Deferred charges and other credits

—Deferred income

—Common and preferred stock carried at issuance price

For example, if a German subsidiary maintains its financial records in U.S. dollars, the statements must be remeasured to the parent company currency.

In the profit and loss statement, cost of sales and depreciation expense will be translated at historical cost, in addition to all other items noted above, as they flow through the income statement. After the financial statements have been "remeasured" using two or more translation rates, there will be an imbalance in the remeasured totals (see Exhibit 3.1). This is due to the varying translation rates used on the previously balanced financial statements.

The balancing adjustment required will affect the current year profit and loss statement, and will be reported as foreign currency remeasurement gains/losses. Note that a change in the current rate from .50/$ to .70/$ results in an additional $320 of profit before tax (PBT). This is due to the increased sales, $540 net of increased expenses of $220.

Translation

Translation is the application of a simple mathematical rule—multiplication of the local currency financial statements by the appropriate translation rate. Since "translation" is simply the result of a multiplication, and has no economic basis for affecting current year earnings, any imbalance from the multiplication will not be considered in the determination of current year earnings. In Exhibit 3.2, we can see that translation" rules require all financial accounts, except equity, to be translated at the current rate. Note that earnings are not as seriously affected by the translation rate change.

Equity represents the accumulation of investment—either capital or retained earnings. These investments should reflect the long-term earning power of the entity. Currency effects, while not necessarily affecting current earnings, should be reflected in the equity value. In Exhibit 3.2, the equity segment of the balance sheet reflects cumulative translation adjustment. Such translation losses are deferred until the specific foreign investment is wholly or substantially liquidated.

Exhibit 3.1
Remeasurement Gains/Losses

($000'S)

DESCRIPTION	LOCAL CURR	: TRANS : RATE	U.S. DOLLAR	: TRANS : RATE	U.S. DOLLAR
CASH	100 :	0.50	50 :	0.70	70
INVENTORY	1000 :	0.45	450 :	0.45	450
ACCOUNTS RECEIVABLE	1500 :	0.50	750 :	0.70	1050
TOTAL ASSETS	2600 :		1250 :		1570
DEBT	1000 :	0.50	500 :	0.70	700
EQUITY	:		:		
CAPITAL STOCK	400 :	0.40	160 :	0.40	160
RETAINED EARNINGS	:		:		
PRIOR PERIOD	1000 :	0.40	400 :	0.40	400
CURRENT PERIOD	200 :	0.50	160 :	0.70	440
TRANSLATION ADJUSTMENT	:		30 :		-130
TOTAL LIABILITIES & EQUITY	2600 :		1250 :		1570
SALES	2700 :	0.50	1350 :	0.70	1890
COST OF SALES-@ STANDARD	1200 :	0.50	600 :	0.70	840
= - HIST		-0.05	-60	-0.25	-300
GROSS PROFIT	1500 :		810 :		1350
S.G.& A. EXPENSES	1100 :	0.50	550 :	0.70	770
PROFIT BEFORE TAX	400 :		260 :	0.70	580
PROFIT AFTER TAX	200 :		160 :	0.70	440

Translation should not be confused with the monetary "transaction gain/loss" required for current liabilities (e.g., accounts payable, in other than the functional currency). If a U.S. company owed 10,000 Deutsch Marks (DMs) and the DM value moved from 2 to the dollar to 3 to the dollar, there would be a real economic gain. The U.S. dollar equivalent of the DM payable would decline from $5000 to $3333.33, and a transaction gain of $1667 would be recorded in the current year P&L.

RESPONSIBILITY REPORTING

The technical accounting aspects of reporting in an international organization have already been reviewed. One of the primary objectives

Exhibit 3.2
Example: Financial Statement Translation

($000'S)

DESCRIPTION	LOCAL CURR	: TRANS : RATE	U.S. DOLLAR	: TRANS : RATE	U.S. DOLLAR
		:		:	
CASH	100	: 0.5	50	: 0.7	70
INVENTORY	1000	: 0.5	500	: 0.7	700
ACCOUNTS RECEIVABLE	1500	: 0.5	750	: 0.7	1050
TOTAL ASSETS	2600	:	1300	:	1820
		:		:	
DEBT	1000	: 0.5	500	: 0.7	700
EQUITY		:		:	
CAPITAL STOCK	400	: 0.4	160	: 0.4	160
		:		:	
RETAINED EARNINGS		:		:	
PRIOR PERIOD	1000	: 0.4	400	: 0.4	400
CURRENT PERIOD	200	: 0.5	100	: 0.7	140
TRANSLATION ADJUSTMENT		:	140	:	420
TOTAL LIABILITIES & EQUITY	2600	:	1300	:	1820
SALES	2700	: 0.5	1350	: 0.7	1890
COST OF SALES	1200	: 0.5	600	: 0.7	840
GROSS PROFIT	1500	:	750	:	1050
		:		:	
S.G.& A. EXPENSES	1100	: 0.5	550	: 0.7	770
PROFIT BEFORE TAX	400	: 0.5	200	: 0.7	280
PROFIT AFTER TAX	200	: 0.5	100	: 0.7	140

of reporting is to communicate the status of operating results to management. This can be done using a traditional set of financial statements (see Exhibit 3.1), or through preparation of reports modified to provide the status of results compared to established guidelnes.

Factors which should be considered in the development of responsibility reporting include:

1. Clear definition of specific responsibilities. These should include definition of product line responsibilities, geographic responsibilities, foreign currency effects (including the effects of FASB 52 and the economic effects of foreign exchange variances on a foreign entity).
2. Frequency of reporting to ensure proper level of control.
3. Content and preparation of the reporting. Reports must clearly and concisely present the results of operations to ensure that the proper level of management can interpret the results.

Definition of Responsibility

International operations can be more easily controlled if responsibilities have been properly defined. Although budget responsibility will be discussed more thoroughly in another chapter, the basic concepts will be presented here. In addition to the customary sales, earnings, and asset control measures, factors that must be considered in the measurement and definition of international goals include:

1. Responsibility for remeasurement gains/losses, which may not be controllable by foreign operations. (This could also be referred to as translation gains/losses.)
2. Responsibility for transaction gains/losses. These are generally due to changes in currency rates on cash equivalents (accounts receivable, accounts payable, etc.).
3. Responsibility for effects on sales and earnings resulting from fluctuations in foreign exchange rates.
4. Impact on operations due to severe changes in local, political, or economic areas.

Each of these items can have a significant impact on operations and performance decisions. As such, the responsibilities must be analyzed thoroughly to ensure that proper organization goals are established. Remeasurement gains/losses and transaction gains/losses are easily quantified and conceptually simple to grasp. Currency variance effects on operating results due to changing sales values and resulting earnings variances are more difficult to quantify.

Exhibit 3.3 highlights some of the significant management adjustments that may be reflected in reported results. Recall that local currency results do not change (in the short term) due to the currency changes, while reported U.S. dollar earnings vary substantially. The impact on operating results should be thoroughly understood to ensure that proper reporting and financial performance measurement against goals are completed. Management should prepare sensitivity analyses, based on possible rate changes, to understand the foreign exchange impact on forecasted results.

Examples of improper definition of responsibility are:

Offshore sales and earnings are budgeted in constant U.S. dollars.

In stable periods there will no impact on performance or decision making if constant dollars are used. If rates fluctuate significantly during the year, local sales, costs, and expenses will be theoretically unaffected by the changes in rates, but U.S. dollar reporting may be seriously affected. (See Exhibits 3.1 and 3.2.)

Exhibit 3.3
Management Adjustment Factors

	Local Currency	Budget Trans Rate	Remeas Impact	Fx Impact	Transl Adjust	Total U.S. Dollars
Sales	2700	1350		135		1485
Cost of Sales	1200	600	20	60		680
Gross Profit	1500	750	20	75		805
SG & A Expense	1100	550		55	20	625
Profit Before Tax	400	200	-20	20	-20	180
Profit After Tax	200	100	-10	10	-10	90

All products sold by the subsidiary are priced in U.S. dollars, with prolonged terms. Subsidiary management cannot hedge foreign currency exposures.

In this situation, the foreign operation can experience large transaction gains or losses with no possible compensation for the transaction effects. Responsibility should be defined to ensure that the subsidiary has either both the responsibility and the authority to respond to the market, or no responsibility for transaction effects.

Report Format/Content

Format and content are as important as definition of responsibility. Basic reports should be submitted periodically to ensure that effective operating control is maintained. However, summarizing the reporting to reflect the matrix of information is complex. A uniform currency must be selected to properly consolidate the information. Assuming the currency is the U.S. dollar, how can we develop a simple summary, identifying all the unusual management information required? Exhibits 3.4 and 3.5 present simple solutions to the presentation of the information matrix. Information for these exhibits is developed from standard reports (full P&L and balance sheet) submitted by the subsidiaries.

Remeasurement G(L) and the translation adjustment were described earlier. A new concept presented in the exhibit is F/X impact. This value relates to the foreign exchange impact on the local currency statements, when compared to an established base—for example, budget or prior year. For example, if the exchange rate moves from .75/U.S.$ to .5/U.S.$, the impact on the P&L is as follows:

	Local	U.S. Dollars @.75	U.S. Dollars @.5
Sales	1000	750	500
Gross profit	500	375	250
SG&A	300	225	150
PBT	200	150	100

In the short term, sales and earnings variances may result from these currency variances. Headquarters management must determine if the off-shore management should be considered responsible for the effect. Remember that this variance could result in substantial gains as well, and should be reviewed for potential higher returns to the company. Therefore, it should definitely be monitored to ensure proper performance measurement.

Exhibit 3.4
Net Earnings: Managerial Statements

COUNTRY	NET EARNINGS	:	U.S. EXPENSE	REMEAS G(L)	F/X IMPACT	TRANSL ADJUST	INTERCO PROFIT	:	ADJUSTED EARNINGS
AUSTRIA		:						:	
FRANCE		:						:	
GERMANY		:						:	
ITALY		:						:	
NETHERLANDS		:						:	
SPAIN		:						:	
SWEDEN		:						:	
SWITZERLAND		:						:	
EUROPE		:						:	
AUSTRALIA		:						:	
HONG KONG		:						:	
JAPAN		:						:	
KOREA		:						:	
SINGAPORE		:						:	
FAR EAST		:						:	
ARGENTINA		:						:	
BRAZIL		:						:	
MEXICO		:						:	
PANAMA		:						:	
PUERTO RICO		:						:	
LATIN AMERICA		:						:	
U.S. EXPENSES		:						:	
F/X IMPACT		:						:	
TRANSLATION G/L		:						:	
INTERCO PROFIT		:						:	
TOTAL INTERNATIONAL		:	0	0	0	0	0	:	

1. Remeasurement G(L) represents gains/losses as a result of remeasuring
   the financial statements from the functional currency in the
   given local currency.

2. F/X impact represents the U.S. dollar variance to budget/prior year
   based on the change in foreign exchange translation rates.

3. Translation adjustment represents the effects of foreign exchange
   gains/losses on liabilities and assets denominated in currencies
   other than the functional currency.

Exhibit 3.5
Sales Reporting: Managerial Statements

COUNTRY	SALES	:	U.S. SALES	INTERCO	F/X IMPACT	NEW PRODUCT	DISCONT PRODUCT	:	ADJUSTED SALES
AUSTRIA		:						:	
FRANCE		:						:	
GERMANY		:						:	
ITALY		:						:	
NETHERLANDS		:						:	
SPAIN		:						:	
SWEDEN		:						:	
SWITZERLAND		:						:	
EUROPE		:						:	
AUSTRALIA		:						:	
HONG KONG		:						:	
JAPAN		:						:	
KOREA		:						:	
SINGAPORE		:						:	
FAR EAST		:						:	
ARGENTINA		:						:	
BRAZIL		:						:	
MEXICO		:						:	
PANAMA		:						:	
PUERTO RICO		:						:	
LATIN AMERICA		:						:	
U.S. SALES		:						:	
F/X IMPACT		:						:	
NEW PRODUCT		:						:	
DISCONTINUED PRODUCT		:						:	
TOTAL INTERNATIONAL		:	0	0	0	0	0	:	

Exhibit 3.4 represents one method of preparing full disclosure statements to identify factors affecting net earnings. This format can be used to identify currency effects or any other managerial adjustments considered necessary. In Exhibit 3.4 earnings are summarized by region. Adjustments are represented as separate columns as well as lines in the schedule. This simple, self-balancing statement will provide a quick basis for review, identifying any management issues requiring analysis.

Exhibit 3.5 reflects similar adjustment columns for managerial review of sales. Such a format can be used to effectively disclose a "matrix" of responsibility. The information is extracted from basic financial statements submitted by offshore units.

If performance objectives are not properly established, local management could be subjected to unusual stress to deliver earnings without the ability to influence performance.

Items which should be thoroughly reviewed to ensure equitable responsibility assignments include:

Remeasurement gains/losses

Transaction gains/losses

Currency impact — Sales
                   — Cost of sales
                   — Expenses

Asset levels — Inventory
              — Accounts receivable
              — Capital assets

Liabilities — Loans payable
            — Accounts payable

These areas generally represent factors that could be serious control issues to offshore management during periods of significant currency fluctuation.

Responsibility for geographic regions and/or product lines should be developed to ensure that all operating risks have been considered and assigned to responsible management.

Reporting Frequency

Companies frequently develop a routine for reporting that may require weekly, monthly, or quarterly reporting. Reporting should be completed only to the extent that action will result from the report. Reports should not be developed unless the information represents business information that will be used by management. Examples of reports and their frequency follow:

	Responsibility Reporting		
	Local	Regional	Int'l
Weekly			
Sales	X	X	X
T&E	X		
Cash flow	X	X	X
Monthly			
Sales	X	X	X
Gross profit	X	X	X
Operating expenses	X	X	X
Cash flow	X	X	X

Accounts receivable	X	X	X
Inventory	X	X	X
Capital requests	X	X	X
Manpower	X	X	X
Sales statistics	X	X	X
Quarterly			
Balance sheet			
Deferred expense	X	X	X
Capital additions	X	X	X

Note that weekly reports are limited. Sales, T&E, and cash flow may be critical management factors in an organization. Matrix reporting (see Exhibit 3.5) could be used to report all critical factors and the bases for measurement to international management.

SUMMARY

It is extremely difficult to be successful in international operations, and it is even more difficult to explain successful operations to management. International operations management requires an awareness of all facets of normal business, the added dimension of foreign currency effects, and the translation impact of FASB 52. Management must be aware of the typical pitfalls of business—personnel, marketing, distribution, sales, accounting, and business planning—and must also manage in a continuously changing environment. Typical ground rules do not apply.

By developing an awareness of the unusual financial features in the international environment, management can improve its effectiveness. Unusual features must be singled out for review and analysis and used as the basis for improved decision making. This chapter has briefly presented accounting standards and discussed some of the more common failures of international management. Proper goal setting and periodic measurement through well-developed financial summaries will result in improved overall management performance.

CHAPTER 4

ORGANIZATION AND STRUCTURE: THE HEADQUARTERS FUNCTION AND STAFFING

International operations headquarters require specific structures to be successful in the management of a dynamic, worldwide operation. Frequently these will take the same form as a typical U.S. management pyramid. However, many times these structures need to meet the unusual demands of the headquarters personnel. Headquarters (HQ) personnel have unusual responsibilities as worldwide leaders and technical experts in their fields. At a minimum, they are policy setters. Many offshore employees may also believe that HQ individuals know all U.S. personnel as well as everything about all phases of the worldwide operation.

If this is believed by the offshore personnel, it must be considered in the definition of the organization structure and the selection of the HQ personnel. HQ personnel can function best if given proper overall direction, specific responsibilities, and the ability to respond to questions posed by offshore personnel. This chapter will discuss many of the keys to successful definition of the organization, a guideline for defining the HQ charter, and principles for selection of HQ personnel. All functions (e.g., marketing, finance) need not be staffed immediately, but should be considered in the initial staff outline. At the completion of this chapter, the reader should be better prepared to develop, through careful consideration, an international operating staff which should accommodate a dynamic, growing operation. After initial staff planning is complete, the chapter can serve as a guideline for further development through periodic organizational review and updating.

THE CHARTER

A charter is a definition of the corporate performance guidelines for an international HQ unit. General responsibilities and duties as well as broad guidelines for performance should be defined. The charter should establish the tone for the HQ personnel. An example of an international HQ charter would be as follows:

The international headquarters will consist of a group of individuals who are familiar with or are *functional specialists*, who have exceptional *communication ability*, and are willing to *deliver results*. The headquarters' responsibility is to *function as a team* to deliver overall international results. This will be accomplished through frequent and routine contact with other headquarters personnel and frequent positive contact with the offshore operations. The goal of the headquarters staff is to perform in a *positive, supportive* role for the offshore subsidiaries, while maintaining a *properly controlled* business environment.

Note that several areas in the above charter have been emphasized. These areas represent the most important considerations in charter definition.

Depending on the stage of development, functional specialties must be considered in the headquarters' function. At a minimum, the following specialties should be considered: sales, marketing, accounting/finance, personnel, distribution, and manufacturing. The basis for selecting specialties is an analysis of the business operation and the development status of the international organization.

Communication ability is essential. Assuming that offshore international operations are staffed by nationals, effective communication skills are essential for all members of the HQ staff.

If it is easy to develop simple excuses for ineffective performance in the United States, consider all the possible excuses for poor performance in the international environment! All HQ personnel must have an intense desire to deliver the results.

In that international HQ is the focal point of all international activity, each member of the HQ must contribute responsibly to the overall effort. Recall that international personnel represent the HQ for all functional disciplines, not just their specialties. HQ personnel must be willing to serve as liaisons for any questions that may arise. HQ personnel must act as a single functioning unit, and the results must reflect this effort.

HQ personnel have no direct impact in the market. However, their support is essential to the company's efforts to win out against competitors. Within specific boundaries—that is, the corporate charter—they must provide the necessary support to achieve the company's targets.

Thus far we have discussed the positive or developmental approach to the headquarters' environment. However, it is essential that international operations are properly managed. It is critical that this diversified, multinational offshore force be effectively controlled. This may apply to financial performance, project control, or programmed sales/marketing efforts. HQ is responsible for the continuous reinforcement of the ethical standards and business sense that the company maintains.

It is the division or international president who establishes the charter and ensures that all international personnel understand their role. Implementation of the charter will vary, depending on the stage of development of the particular international organization. For example, in a new organization, the charter should be implemented immediately, establishing operating policy. In an existing organization, the charter concept should be introduced immediately, but the implementation should be paced to avoid unreasonable organizational stress. Change may be difficult, depending on the tenacity of habits developed by existing HQ personnel.

HEADQUARTERS ORGANIZATION

Regional Versus Functional Structure

After a charter has been established, the company must determine the best method for organizing the HQ operation. Remember that eventually all organizations result in a pyramid structure.

Functional responsibilities must be carefully evaluated since the HQ is the focal point for worldwide coordination. Initially, in newly formed international operations, specialties may not be as critical as decisiveness, trustworthiness, and general competence. Organizations may require less specialty when sales volumes and business risks are smaller. It may be difficult to substantiate an investment in HQ for a full range of specialists when offshore operations have total sales less than $25 to $50 million. With these sales volumes, specialties should be invested in major offshore or rapidly developing offshore operations. As the offshore units define procedures to resolve manufacturing/distribution marketing questions, the HQ personnel should communicate the solutions to other operations. In effect, the specialties in the larger subsidiaries will be "multiplied" through the HQ functions.

In Exhibit 4.1, ellipses are used to represent organizational requirements. These shapes are descriptive of the types of organizations needed. For example, if a company has 15 subsidiaries, with a total sales of $60 million, HQ organization may be directed toward specialities. Since the subsidiaries are relatively small, highly trained, seasoned specialists may not be available in the offshore operation. This need must then be satisfied by HQ staff. Also, if the organization has 15 subsidiaries and $400 million sales, specialists are again required. But these specialists are policy setters, familiar with the requirements of specialized areas, for example

Exhibit 4.1
Organizational Requirements

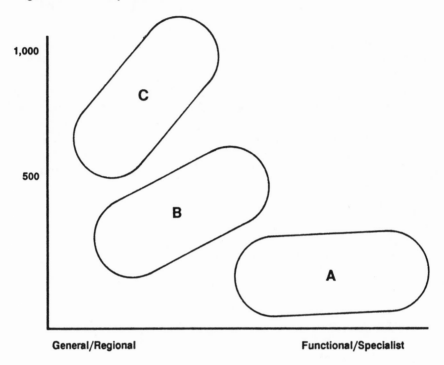

A = Rapidly developing, small offshore operations;
    similar business problems.

B = Generally well established; moderate development;
    generally larger operations; either staffed or able
    to afford consultants.

C = Well established large offshore operations; regional
    specialties required due to close working relationships.
    Locally staffed with specialists.

manufacturing engineering. The sheer magnitude of the investment requires a coordinator/policy setter to ensure smooth business operation. These HQ staff will be management level employees to ensure that appropriate decisions are made. Detail work and development of proposals should be completed at the subsidiary.

Another organizational consideration is the regional knowledge required for proper functioning. The question of regional versus functional is a theoretical question, since most organizations contain a mixture of both. For example, at its limit, a region could be as small as a subsidiary management team.

The regional concept provides a basis for a close working relationship between HQ and the offshore operations. Specific regions of the world will have unique operating characteristics. Regional contacts or expertise may be essential to proper development of regional operations. Regional organizations are decision oriented, with minimal technical support from HQ.

Functional organization will be aligned with functional responsibilities (e.g., marketing or personnel). This alignment will provide concentrated functional expertise to support offshore operations. The objective of a functional organization is to perform service for the offshore operations. Effectively, a functional organization competes with local consultants or local specialists who could provide individual services to subsidiaries.

These two types of organization must be balanced to properly develop international operations. Note in Exhibit 4.2 that the type of organization must be adjusted periodically, based on the size and diversity of the

Exhibit 4.2
Organizational Balance

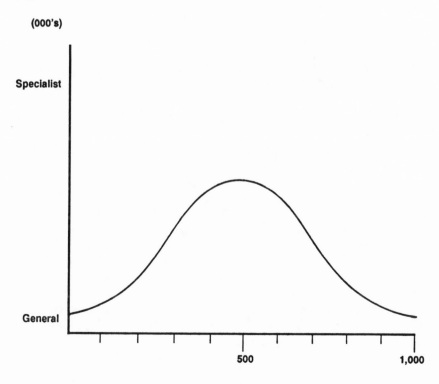

operation. This is essential since a full matrix organization (i.e., a combination of functional and regional) is not economically feasible in many organizations. The HQ should be periodically evaluated to ensure that there is a proper balance between "specialists" and "generalists." Balancing an existing organization should be done carefully to avoid disrupting both HQ and offshore operations.

Initially the regional specialty should be the focal point of the operation since understanding the particular market is the basis for development of larger subsidiaries. As offshore operations expand, emphasis on the functional aspects of the operation within the subsidiaries must be developed. This results from larger, more complex operations, requiring on-site expertise. As offshore operations become more successful and individual local decisions become more complex, "generalists" in the headquarters are required to evaluate policy level decisions. Detailed knowledge must be gained at the offshore location to ensure that the proper decision is being made. The subsidiary is the first line of defense against poor decision making.

Definition of Headquarters Responsibility

In either organization the HQ staff should understand that a dual responsibility exists. HQ must provide service/counsel to the largest customers of the U.S. company (each offshore subsidiary), and must ensure that parent company policies are adhered to and that decisions implemented are in the best interest of the company.

HQ personnel must be the policy setters, disciplinarians, and counselors for each offshore unit. Recall that each offshore unit has full operational requirements, and must properly consider all major business disciplines in its subsidiary: marketing, finance, human resources, material control and distribution, and sales.

HQ personnel must review the needs of offshore companies, and determine the best counsel for subsidiary success. The difficult part of this responsibility is that periodically the offshore unit may not understand either existing or potential problems. As a result, the HQ personnel may develop directives unique to the offshore unit to ensure that proper strategic development is achieved. Offshore subsidiaries may concentrate so heavily on routine responsibilities that they may fail to identify strategic business needs.

For example, consider a technically advanced product line, where a continuous stream of new products is expected during the next one to two years. Business is expected to double in the next twelve months. HQ personnel may have been involved in such growth situations historically, while subsidiary management may not have such experience. Using the HQ experience, a proper organizational structure may be developed for the expected growth, but to the apparent detriment of the current year earnings. HQ personnel must assist the offshore management team in developing the proper structure with appropriate personnel and job descriptions, without resorting to a "directive" approach. There must be an experience transfer from the HQ personnel to the offshore team.

It is difficult to prove that HQ has assisted in the proper management of the subsidiary. HQ must provide this counsel through frequent positive guidance and feedback. This may also take on the "directive" role when operations are not being managed properly. The most important consideration of the HQ staff is to provide support for the offshore operation, yet remain nearly invisible. In other words, HQ staff should ensure that proper decisions are made and represent the parent company's best interest, always remembering that effective decisions are made by the subsidiary management team.

The subsidiary management teams should be well qualified, trained, and experienced professionals who are fully capable of managing a business. Offshore staff should be allowed to manage under expert guidance.

The strategic balance of the HQ organization should be reviewed annually to ensure that the existing structure matches the current need. This should be completed in a systematic way, considering the evolution of the offshore operations as well as offshore business needs.

Headquarter's decision making. As with many other management situations, the best decisions are those completed by the individuals responsible for implementing them. In the international environment, decisions should be made by the offshore unit. Headquarters' "remote control" decision making may not be an unusual management technique in international operations but this could be a serious mistake, since the best information and the first line of defense against poor decisions is in the field. If decisions are continuously forced from HQ with little input from offshore teams (e.g., if it worked in Chicago, it must be workable in Rome) we may find deteriorating morale and subsidiary management that will be reluctant to make decisions. The best decisions made will be finalized by the offshore personnel, based on HQ counsel.

The HQ staff should represent the best interest of the major "stockholder"—the parent company. Counsel from the HQ will provide the necessary perspective for the offshore management to better interpret the needs of the parent company. Occasionally, actions may be taken to the detriment of the offshore subsidiary, but to the benefit of the parent company. Offshore personnel should understand their role in the organization. While general informal guidelines may be developed, it is important to have firm written policies available for review and reference by the offshore personnel. A primary function of the HQ staff is to prepare and interpret the guidelines, and to provide the rationale for the decisions resulting from the guidelines. The HQ personnel must establish rapport with offshore personnel to ensure the trust necessary to function effectively. This can be accomplished through frequent positive contact, and counsel and written opinions when required.

Communication responsibility. The HQ communication system is complicated, due to the service/client relationship that must permeate the international HQ function. Note in Exhibit 4.3 that communication should be concentrated in the HQ in order to maintain control. This becomes difficult due to the number of contacts made and the number of specialties necessary. If for any reason the offshore personnel determine that the HQ people are working for personal gain or advantage, much of their advice will be discarded. Communication should be predetermined and regularly scheduled, not merely "spur-of-the moment." Frequent communication with the offshore operations will ensure the openness required in case unusual events occur.

The HQ staff must cultivate routine communication—that is, specific, periodic contact with offshore personnel. Such communication should include offshore information that is used at the HQ, and information that allows HQ personnel to understand that the offshore operation is being successfully managed.

Exhibit 4.3A
Communication Matrix: Functional Organization

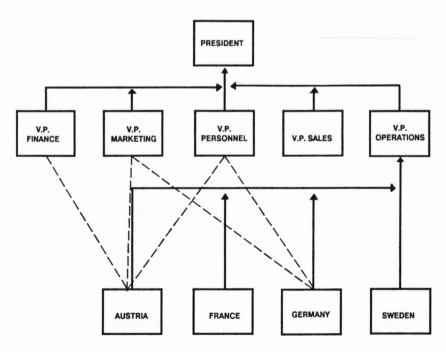

Exhibit 4.3B
Communication Matrix: Regional Orientation

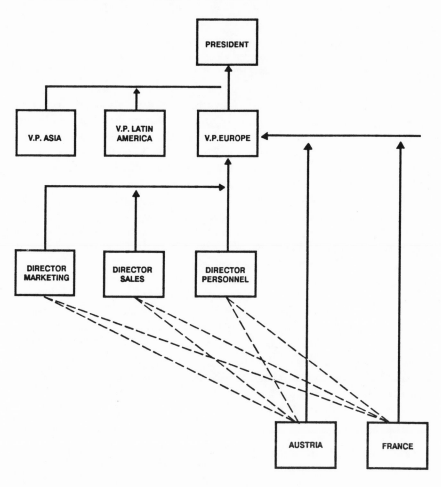

However, the communication process must be managed. HQ personnel must conscientiously review communication needs, developing a routine reporting structure and a trust relationship with the offshore personnel to ensure timely communication of any critical business information.

FUNCTIONS TO BE CONSIDERED

Definition of Needs

Establishing the HQ staff is a business decision to be carefully considered, based on definition of needs. Generally, all operations require people to operate, and each subsidiary will sell a tangible product or intangible service.

Subsidiaries perform in certain distribution channels (e.g., retail, wholesale, government, educational, other institutional, etc.). Some of these channels will be highly competitive, others relatively dormant. Technology may be critical in the product offering. This must be considered in the definition of the HQ.

In effect, all areas of the marketing mix must be considered in the proper definition of the HQ staff. The analysis must consider the reliance on the corporation's centralized functions (any function performed in the corporation's host country—e.g., the United States), the "time-distance" multiple for HQ service, and the individual skills in each of the offshore units. This is essential since all subsidiaries are not equal. They may be of differing size, maturity, and stage of development.

Exhibit 4.4 demonstrates a method for evaluating HQ needs. Note that the matrix is similar to the marketing needs matrix developed in chapter 13. This example, however, is segregated into alternate decision groups (e.g., manufacturing, distribution, personnel, etc.). These groupings will be helpful for determining the company's use of consultants, which will be discussed later.

The HQ requirements definition must consider the main components of all business operations, such as personnel, manufacturing/distribution, marketing, and finance/accounting. These functions represent the keys to all operations—the proper management of the "people" resource and the product resource (either manufacturing or distribution). Of course, without effective control and reporting, the company would not be aware of meeting these objectives. Finance/accounting becomes critical to ensure that effective control reporting is completed.

Personnel. This function considers current organizational needs based on thorough analysis of the business operation. Factors such as organizational depth (professional staffing compared to clerical or nonprofessional), job training, succession planning, and strategic personnel planning must be considered annually to ensure that the organization is at the proper stage of development to suit business needs. Remember, the final product can be delivered only through close coordination of offshore personnel.

Manufacturing/distribution. Manufacturing/distribution requires immediate attention so that a proper level of service is offered offshore. If the business is a service operation, the intangible product may require closer attention by "functional specialists."

Marketing. Marketing represents the most complete of the functional specialties. Effective marketing considers product, price, place, and promotion. Each of these variables affects personnel, manufacturing/distribution, and reporting against objectives. Effective marketing can result in successful performance. Ineffective marketing may result in disastrous losses.

Exhibit 4.4
Headquarters Requirements Definition

Responsibility	AUSTRIA		GERMANY		NETHERLNDS		SWEDEN		SWITZ		EUROPE	
	Req	Avail	Req	Avail	Req	Avail	Req	Avail	Req	Avail	Req	Avail
Personnel												
Organization planning												
Succession planning												
Bonus/compensation planning												
Professional training												
Pension planning												
Union negotiations												
Labor board review												
Manufacturing												
Engineering support-												
Product development												
Product enhancement												
MRP Planning												
MRP Installation												
MRP Maintenance												
Cost accounting systems												
Lot control systems												
Procurement												
Marketing												
Product design												
Product development												
Market research												
Market planning - annual												
Market planning - strategic												
Pricing administration												
Advertising development												
Advertising copy												
Media control												

Finance/accounting. If all other functions have been properly considered, a successful business will require effective record keeping and planning. The finance function provides a disciplined basis for preparing summaries of actual performance and projections of future performance. Finance personnel at their best will integrate the needs of personnel, manufacturing, and marketing to ensure an effective financial communication system.

The HQ requirements definition can be created only through a thorough analysis of the operations requirements. That is, the individuals responsible for the international performance must define their requirements. These requirements must be carefully considered, since they will define the organization for at least one year and perhaps more.

Use of Consultants

After the HQ requirements definition has been completed, it is necessary to respond to it. It is unlikely that an operation will be able to support the requirements definition fully from internal sources. It then becomes necessary to extensively analyze the costs of supporting the needs. Consultants are available in every country, in every specialty at any time. The only factors that must be seriously considered in the selection of consultants are their capability and the cost. It may seem optimistic that a consultant is available anytime needed, but think about the requirement. Availability may require the consultant to travel nine hours from Rio de Janeiro to Belem, Brazil. But the consultant is available.

The HQ requirements definition should define the specialty required and the frequency. After the basics have been defined, cost estimates should be obtained for the defined support services and decisions made. Some consultants may actually be from within a company, but with other divisions. Consultants can also be licensed professionals (attorneys or CPAs) or financial experts (bankers) obtained locally. Exhibit 4.5 provides an example of a consultant analysis. Consultant references can be obtained from local banks, international accounting and law firms, trade associations, and local chambers of commerce.

Personality Traits

Each contact with offshore subsidiaries represents a limited exposure to the HQ. HQ personnel must be mature enough to wield power sensibly. Traits that should be carefully considered in the selection of HQ personnel include:

1. *Maturity.* As discussed earlier, maturity, or the ability to handle power effectively, is essential. The HQ representatives have implied power through their

Exhibit 4.5
Financial Analysis: Consultants

Description of Task:

Country/region	Estimated Hours	Rate	Est Cost	(A) Full Service	(B) Incremental Cost	(C) "Skip"

A) Salary/Fringe
   Travel
   O/H - @ _____ %

B) Travel and Entertainment

C) "Skip" - Potential losses

close association with all international executives. Prudent use of power is essential for all international personnel.

2. *Technical ability/breadth.* HQ personnel must be technical experts in their chosen specialties, since the HQ is the policy setting body of the organization. This does not necessarily mean that the individual knows all facts related to a specialty, but that the person can intelligently discuss pertinent matters with local specialists. Breadth of background is essential since each HQ member fully represents the HQ at each contact with the subsidiary. If the person does not know the answer, he must be able to understand the question and properly relate it to a responsible HQ person.

3. *Expert communication ability.* The HQ person must be an expert communicator. It is important to understand that most offshore personnel may have a different native language than the HQ. Effective communication means an expert listener as well as communicator. Limited contact with the HQ may mean that the offshore group will use each opportunity with the HQ to speak about all business considerations. They expect to be understood with minimal effort.

4. *Teaching ability.* The HQ staff must be willing teachers. They must be committed to delivering guidance at the pace dictated by the training of offshore personnel. The HQ must be able to define objectives and know the background of objectives to explain their development to the offshore management. They must be willing to redirect the effort of the offshore management team in a positive way. Dedication to this purpose is essential.

5. *High energy level.* HQ personnel potentially deal with all time zones of the world. This may require communication with offshore operations at unusual times of day or on holidays. HQ personnel must be willing to respond in a positive, energetic way to all inquiries.

6. *Team player.* All members of the HQ operation must be team players, concerned with delivering the results. It is not enough to simply do assigned tasks well. All HQ personnel must be enthusiastic and willing to work with all members of the HQ to ensure success.

Each of these traits is essential to obtain the maximum benefit from the HQ operation. Existing HQ operations should carefully consider the portfolio of skills available in the HQ. If additional skills are required, training should be provided to ensure success. If personnel are unable to cope with the demands of the HQ function, career counseling should be considered.

SUMMARY

Effective international HQ definition and implementation represents a primary factor in the ultimate success of any international operation. The HQ requires a charter in order to ensure that proper responsibilities are assumed and duties are performed.

The charter must consider the needs of the organization, which are constantly changing. Functional or regional concentration must be analyzed to determine the overall emphasis of the HQ. Each type of organization has particular features and serves specific purposes. The roles of the HQ should be defined and may vary in different circumstances. The objectives of the HQ are split between serving the offshore locations in a customer/service relationship, or as the corporate guidance counselor, protecting the interests of the corporation.

Specific functions must be initially considered in the HQ. These relate primarily to people, product, and control of the operation.

HQ personality traits are quite specific, since any unusual aberrations in behavior are multiplied by the diversity of the "receivers"—the offshore personnel. The best managers, and personnel must be in the international operations. The HQ is an extremely challenging area to work in, and it is also exceptionally demanding. International HQ personnel should be better organized and better staffed than comparable domestic HQ staff.

CHAPTER 5

COMMUNICATIONS SYSTEMS

"Communications failure" is an overused cliché—yet it is very true in the international environment. Effective international communication must overcome barriers such as differing business background and education, economic environment, and social and legal environments. Effective communication systems can be developed through sophisticated, technically current satellite communication, telephone, or telex systems. Face-to-face communication can also overcome these barriers. This chapter will discuss the effectiveness of each mode of communication, and also provide an in-depth framework for developing a communication plan. Practical examples will be given to ensure that the reader can implement the concepts discussed.

To be successful in international communication, management must control the individuals who communicate, as well as define the content and frequency of communication with offshore personnel. Effective communication must be planned and conscientiously administered to ensure that international operations are properly controlled. This chapter will concentrate on the *who, when, what,* and *how* of communications.

THE COMMUNICATIONS AUDIT

It is difficult to determine answers to the above questions before we determine the environment. In any existing international environment, established communications customs exist. Before we attempt to make improvements, it is essential to understand the current environment. The most effective method of determining the environment is to complete a communications audit.

The communications audit is simply a review and compilation of existing communication. Exhibit 5.1 represents such a simple compilation.

Exhibit 5.1
Example: Communications Audit

Monthly Report

	Austria		Canada		England		Japan		Korea	
	URGENT	ROUTINE	URGENT	ROUTINE	URGENT	ROUTINE	URGENT	ROUTINE	URGENT	ROUTINE
Finance		1		1		1		1		1
Marketing										
Advertising										
Legal										
Patent										
Operations								1		1
Distribution	2			1	3					
Professional Services										

Telephone

	Austria		Canada		England		Japan		Korea	
	URGENT	ROUTINE	URGENT	ROUTINE	URGENT	ROUTINE	URGENT	ROUTINE	URGENT	ROUTINE
Finance										
Marketing	4		2		6		12			
Advertising										
Legal										
Patent										
Operations	15		1		4		15			
Distribution										2
Professional Services										

Telex

	Austria		Canada		England		Japan		Korea	
	URGENT	ROUTINE	URGENT	ROUTINE	URGENT	ROUTINE	URGENT	ROUTINE	URGENT	ROUTINE
Finance	7	3	6	3	4	2	1	2	5	
Marketing										
Advertising										
Legal			2				1			
Patent										
Operations	3		8				3			
Distribution								1		3
Professional Services										

54

Telefax

Finance
Marketing
Advertising
Legal
Patent
Operations
Distribution
Professional Services

Mail (express)

Finance
Marketing
Advertising
Legal
Patent
Operations
Distribution
Professional Services

Mail (Regular)

Finance
Marketing
Advertising
Legal
Patent
Operations
Distribution
Professional Services

Note that the summary identifies key functional areas, communication frequency, and mode of communication. The summary should be prepared periodically during the year to determine if, on an ongoing basis, the communication plan is being achieved. The communication audit should not be a major event, but rather a simple monitoring of existing communication. If the audit is completed at the proper frequency and depth, more effective communication will result. The audit should be done at least twice a year, with results presented to the director of operations.

WHO SHOULD COMMUNICATE?

Many international managers and executives consider the organization chart in the headquarters to be consistent with the perceptions of the offshore personnel. One of the realities of international operations is that headquarters personnel may represent higher levels of authority to the offshore personnel than is apparent in the organization chart. For example, clerical personnel in the headquarters operations may have frequent and authoritative contact with the offshore personnel. This may lead the offshore personnel to believe that these people are responsible for decision making. This may occur in situations such as materials management, marketing, advertising, treasury, financial planning, and accounting.

It is important to understand that offshore personnel may not necessarily understand the U.S. headquarters organization chart. Training, updated organization charts, and specific guidelines for formal communication with offshore personnel should be established in the U.S. headquarters. The training should be given to all personnel who have periodic or frequent communication with the offshore personnel. Training should include:

—A thorough understanding of all offshore subsidiaries (products, services offered, distribution channels countries served)

—Complete lists of the headquarters organization, including names and positons of all personnel, should be available to all international operations people. This is not to imply that higher level people in the offshore operations will receive preferential treatment; an offshore general manager should receive a more prompt response than clerical support in an offshore marketing department.

—Phone personnel should treat each of the offshore operations as though they were the most important customers of the operations.

—It is often helpful to understand how the offshore office looks. A photo album of personnel and operations should be available for review.

"Who" should communicate also depends on the topics covered. Suitable, fixed communications channels should be established, which identify specific personnel for specific topics.

WHEN TO COMMUNICATE

Priorities

It is important to establish priorities for communication with offshore personnel. Prioritizing can be completed automatically, based on offshore position or topics covered. Many times communications that are considered urgent by offshore personnel may not be significant in the scheme of worldwide operations.

However, if something is essential to offshore personnel, it is important to respond in a timely manner. As a formal guideline, communications between offshore operations and headquarters should be answered *within 48 hours.*

Prioritizing communications and responses is essential because of the number and extent of communications required to properly run an international operation. Communications can be both planned and impromptu. Training should allow personnel—both offshore and U.S.—to properly prioritize all communications. Coordination of the communications audit should detect the company's communication strengths/weaknesses and system of prioritizing.

Timing of Responses

Communications timing in international operations may be critical, due to the time zone impact in most international communications. If all offshore communications are considered to be communications with prime customers, response time to communicate will likely be accelerated. It is important to understand that headquarters personnel has as its primary task coordination with offshore personnel to ensure that business is managed successfully. As noted above, response timing is critical. All written correspondence should be date stamped. A formal response to offshore communication should not be delayed beyond 48 hours. If a pattern of responses beyond 48 hours is detected in the communications audit, a formal review of the type and content of the communications should be prepared to correct the problems.

It is essential to adhere to the 48-hour guideline, even if the response is as simple as: "Received your telex regarding your order—unable to determine the outcome of the order until 5 days. Will telex status then." This brief telex acknowledges their telex, and also establishes a frame of response. But remember, the sender must adhere to the target communication deadline. If 5 days is unacceptable, they have the opportunity to respond. Both parties are fully informed of priorities and expectations. Closed loop communication is essential to effective international management.

Classification of Communication

In operations as diverse as international ones, multiple locations and personalities require written guidelines to define the basics of the communication policy. Basic guidelines should include:

—Response timing

—Formal approvals listing

—Response channeling (forwarding instructions if specific personnel are unavailable for response)

—Frequency of communication

These guidelines should be established at headquarters level, with the cooperation of offshore personnel. It is important to understand the frequency and content of communication in international operations. A communications audit should be completed to understand the current communication situation. After a thorough review of the existing communication profile, the company should define an optimum profile. Plans should be established to ensure that the optimum is achieved.

Communication channels are the lifeline for international operations. If the communication channels are overused, their effectiveness is diluted. If the communication channels are underused, the result may be "stranded organizations" that do not understand their goals or responsibilities.

Effective communication depends on content, which can be classified as three priorities: A, B, C.

A represents the most important or critical communications occurring at preestablished times, with preestablished format or content. These may include such items as: monthly reports, quarterly forecasts, annual budgets, monthly production orders, and strategic marketing plans.

These communications are represented by smooth curves (in Exhibit 5.2, the A line). Specific audiences are targeted for each of these communications. These communication channels should be established early in the year so that people can manage their work schedules around them.

B communications represent tactical or nonstrategic communication. These could be routine communications (e.g., determining the status of certain orders for product, advertising material or displays, personnel support, etc.). These are considered B items due to their tactical importance. However, it is important to understand that these items are critical to the offshore operations. These items may represent routine communication related to the successful operation of the offshore subsidiary. Occasionally these communications will reach a "crisis" point. As crisis com-

Exhibit 5.2
Communication Wave Theory

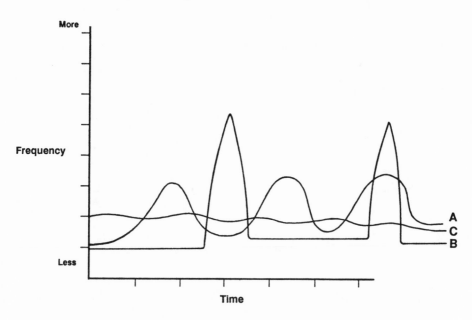

munications become more prevalent, it must be understood that the operation is not functioning as smoothly as it should. This should be an indicator to international management that corrective action or review should be initiated immediately.

C communication represents the least critical of all routine correspondence. It may include general requests about operating procedures in the business environment. Although timing of the response is not critical, guidelines that are established for the organization should be respected. C items may be administrative or organizational guidelines.

WHAT TO COMMUNICATE

What is communicated in the international enviornment is important. It is essential that U.S. headquarters personnel understand that offshore personnel may not be thoroughly trained in the English language. Most U.S.-affiliated offshore companies are staffed by personnel that speak at least two languages, while most U.S. headquarters personnel may speak only one language. This is a common shortcoming of U.S. organizations.

Written communication from offshore personnel may include misused grammar or a poor selection of vocabulary. It is important to avoid criticism of the style, and focus on the content of the communication. Be complimentary of the communication if possible.

The content of the communication will depend on the broad classification (i.e., *A*, *B*, or *C*). *A* communication, as discussed earlier, is pre-established. This may include forms or topics predetermined with management. These reports should include forms or topics predetermined with management. These reports should include items that are critical to the international operations.

It is essential that the headquarters does not request information that does not appear to have a significant or useful purpose.

The request for a report of the offshore operation may reduce time for routine daily operations. The offshore personnel are trying to run a business—dealing with customers, competitors, and government officials. It is important that the business purpose for each communication is understood, so that proper background is prepared by the offshore personnel. A headquarters manager should not be concerned about overcommunicating in this situation. Always be sure that the purpose is understood.

B classification is less structured or defined. This communication is designed to respond to routine business needs. As such, the most critical aspect is to determine the facts required to make decisions. The only factors that should be regimented are individual addressees or approval channels.

C communications are less structured and more administrative in nature. Critical portions of the correspondence are the addressees.

HOW TO COMMUNICATE

Mode of communication should be classified as "written" or "verbal"; (e.g., telephone, "face-to-face"). Mode of communication depends partially on the classification of the communication. Generally *A* and *B* communication should be documented. This is important so that they can be referenced and adequately reviewed by the appropriate personnel in the headquarters and offshore.

Letters are documents that can be reviewed; they can also include nontext material—graphs, pictures, tables, and so on. Letters can be sent by mail requiring up to one month transit time, or by telefax which takes minutes per page. The major decision factor is cost versus results. It may cost hundreds of dollars to transmit a 50-page document by telefax, while a letter could cost only several dollars. If it is critical information, cost is negligible.

Other methods of sending documents include first-class mail, airfreight, or courier service. Courier services operate worldwide and are relatively inexpensive considering the cost of potential delays.

Data-processing electronic mail presents documentary support for all communication. However, such items as pictures and graphic analysis may be difficult to transmit. Telex machines represent immediate communication, postponed only by the requirement to retype or reinput to the telex machine. Cost of the basic telex system is fairly small compared to that of a complete electronic mail data system. Costs would be limited to a network connect charge and machine purchase or rental. Other charges are related only to the volume of data transmitted. Telex use is widespread and represents an inexpensive means of quick, documented communication.

Telecommunications by satellite computer systems represents a major advance during the past decade. Computer networks are economical if large volumes of data are transmitted frequently requiring timely documented evidence at either end. Often data systems are used for transmission of A type reports—extensive financial information or routine periodic reports. Data systems may represent substantial investment for small companies and as a result may be inaccessible. However, "timesharing networks" are available to all operations on a limited cost basis. Investment may be limited to as small an investment as a personal computer, establishing a subscription with a major international network (networks such as GTE Telenet), and connect time for periodic usage. Fortune 100 companies may also establish timesharing networks to market excess time for their own dedicated systems.

SUMMARY

Communications represents such a simple concept that all people seem comfortable discussing it. Communications, however, is a critical part of successful international operations. Communication represents the lifeline for the U.S. headquarters and its offshore operations. Communication includes routine reporting—A items—necessary for the formal routine operations.

Communication audits should be completed to determine if there are inadequacies in the communication network. A routine review should be completed at least annually to determine the timing, content, and mode of communication necessary to successfully monitor international operations. This audit should be completed by management personnel to ensure that the lifeline is intact.

CHAPTER 6

PERSONNEL PLANNING AND THE INTERNATIONAL ENVIRONMENT

Personnel may be one of the most important assets of any organization, yet has no stated value represented on any balance sheet. Individuals who are dedicated to performing high quality service, and who are dedicated to the company are essential for the well-being of the company. These individuals can be located in the United States or offshore.

Since there is both great opportunity for excellent performance and the danger of poor performance, it is essential that the international operation is properly designed and staffed so that all the employees' energy can be devoted to their best performance. The organization must be thoroughly analyzed to ensure that proper skills are available for effective performance, to ensure that appropriate staff levels have been established to generate company success, and to ensure that all levels within the organization have a clear understanding of responsibilities, duties, and adequate supervision.

International operations represent challenging environments, since distance, language, and social differences contribute to the complexities of effective organization. As such, the international environment must be carefully analyzed to ensure that all factors critical to the success of the organization have been considered. It should be noted that this exercise need not be completed immediately or completely, but should be considered periodically to ensure that the organization is at its peak performance.

Offshore personnel represent the greatest potential investments and the greatest potential risks, not because nationals do not perform well, but perhaps because they may not identify with the company. Careful analysis and thorough review of company objectives should reduce this cost in the long term.

THE COMPANY CHARTER

As with the headquarters, the company itself should consider employees' responsibilities and provide broad guidelines for the company's relationship with customers, community, and shareholders. We will review the relationship with employees in this chapter. The charter should be developed by the chief executive of international operations to ensure that it defines appropriate performance requirements.

ORGANIZATION CHARACTERISTICS

Each organization has specific characteristics that must be understood to properly establish a personnel plan. The following sections identify some of the most important characteristics that must be considered to effectively administer an offshore operation.

In each country, characteristics may differ from the basic company characteristics due to local custom or management.

Personality

Each organization has a unique personality. Organizations can appear to be carnivorous, aggressive, ambitious, or conservative. It is necessary to understand the image projected by the existing organization to determine if it is consistent with the desired image. A brief discussion of each type of company will help to better characterize them:

1. *Carnivorous.* Carnivorous companies are defined as companies that have extremely high employee turnover rates and exceptionally aggressive operating targets. These companies are generally in high-tech areas (computers, electronics, pharmaceuticals), and were probably originally "aggressive" companies that modified their long-range goals or simply found "carnivorous" behavior most conducive to prosperity. "Carnivores" may also result from short-term efforts to awaken a conservative company, or to change the style of a company from ambitious to aggressive. This could be a conscious effort or the result of misdirected management efforts. Stress levels in "carnivorous" companies will be high, since performance requirements may be impossibly demanding.

   Rewards for personnel will be extremely high. These companies are generally staffed by young, aggressive individuals who are eager to develop their skills. Long-range prospects for these companies are good, but only if a stream of innovative new products or services are available at regular intervals.

2. *Aggressive.* This organization style is generally found in high technology or modern industry, which also generally have high profit margins. Again elec-

tronics companies, computer, medical technology, and pharmaceutical companies will generally be aggressive. Characteristics of these companies would include demanding requirements for performance, and also probably extremely high rewards. Work tensions and stress would be higher than in a conservative organization—but less than in a carnivore—and should be considered in hiring practices and organization development.

Aggressive organizations are generally staffed by younger (not just in age, but in mental outlook), more aggressive, highly educated individuals. These individuals are interested in quick career growth and "fast-tracking" to the top. Long-range prospects for aggressive companies are healthy, provided a continuous stream of new products or developments is available.

3. *Ambitious.* These companies are closely aligned to "aggressive" companies. Although industries may be similar, many mature product lines may be included in this category. "Ambitious" companies are generally well controlled, with stress factors less than in aggressive companies, yet more than in conservative companies. The "ambitious" label is determined through internally generated goal setting. Effective management (well-educated and mature enough to establish meaningful goals and provide the means to deliver those goals) is necessary to maintain the motivation of an "ambitious" company. An ambitious company can be found in virtually any industry—from mid-tech (such as consumer electronics) to airlines (which have historically been regulated). Rewards in these companies can be generous, since they are based on the success of the operation. "Ambitious" companies can maintain their enthusiasm internally, and will continue to be prosperous. Innovative new products and services are not essential to maintain the "ambitious" status. However, innovative management is critical to the continued success of an ambitious company.

4. *Conservative.* These companies may be extremely large, well-established companies in stable product areas (automobiles, railroads, heavy industry, textiles). Decisions may be slower paced, since the market may not require quick decisions but rather effective decisions. Profit margins overall may be less than in other industries, but may be suitable for long-term prosperity. Internal competition may be reduced, rewards may be smaller for excellent performance. Extensive training and high tech may not be as strong a requirement.

Company personality can be "pegged" due to the industry, but the personality can be changed among offshore operations, based on local management. Change can be accomplished through careful analysis of the current personality, and a clear definition of the personality desired. Although plans to change personality can be easily developed, implementation of the plans may result in organizational stress and eventually require new management. For example, changing from a "sleeping giant" conservative company to an aggressive company may not be practical. The first step would be to an ambitious company.

The graph in Exhibit 6.1 consists of four sections, each with differing stress, educational requirements, and rewards. The graph is not a smooth

Exhibit 6.1
Corporate Personality

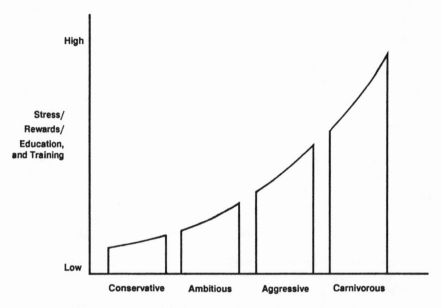

one, because moving from stage to stage increases stress in management, resulting in dropouts. Turmoil may result, even from a small shift from "conservative" to "ambitious" status. It would be extremely difficult to try to develop an "aggressive" personality within a "conservative" company.

A company can move among these characteristic company personalities, recognizing the potential disruption. Also, the company should thoroughly understand its personality to select personnel better to "fit" its personality. International organizations have the opportunity to establish a modified personality at each location since offshore operations may have slightly different personalities than the company, due to prevailing market conditions and local management.

Commitment to Employees

This characteristic is important in the international organization, since each offshore operation is a business that defines its commitment to the employees. Employees in an offshore operation may not recognize the U.S. perception of a "worldwide commitment." Although the company headquarters may have established training programs (e.g., career progression within the company, on-the-job training), this may not be evident in the offshore unit. This should be recognized and programs developed in each offshore operation if the headquarters considers it appropriate.

Commitment to employees can be demonstrated through local development programs (educational seminars, training) or through continuous positive feedback. The company must establish meaningful, achievable goals, and routinely support offshore personnel to ensure that the proper level of commitment is understood by offshore personnel. Other examples of commitment to employees would include a willingness to cross-train for new assignments, or promote from within the international operation.

Dedication to Customer and Product Quality

During the past few years, companies have understood that the customer is essential to company success. Although this may not have been a business basic in the past, the company must be sure that the expected level of customer service is part of its charter. Brochures can be printed and slogans can be developed stating that customer service is a requisite, *but it must be believed in each operation.* Offshore units function directly as the division president dictates. If the standards of customer service are not effectively communicated to offshore units, the company will not succeed within its corporate charter.

Personnel selection and organization must be considered in the overall quality statement. If the organization is not properly staffed, customer service and product quality may be inconsistent with that desired.

ORGANIZATION STRUCTURE

A company's organization structure should reflect the needs of that company. "Needs" can usually be summarized as the organization necessary to provide service to the customer. There are many factors to consider when developing an international organization. Remember that each country or market may have differing requirements.

Market Classification

Company personality in each offshore operation is dependent on the offshore management. The offshore management may vary based on the type of market. There are four main types of markets (see chapter 1): developing markets, maturing markets, matured markets, and undefined markets. Each of these types of market has a different personality. Certain personnel attributes are required of each type of market:

1. *Developing markets.* These companies could very well have the "carnivore" or "aggressive" company style. These companies are generally in control of the

market, with high market share and dominant pricing strategy, and are usually staffed by the most professional employees within the market. "Fast-track" executives, who must deliver the results, and may be demanding, are the norm.

2. *Maturing markets.* These operations may also be staffed by the "best" employees. The character may be less aggressive, since these subsidiaries may be in a more mature phase of their product life cycle. The personnel in these operations will live in a more predictable environment, since stability is one of the features of maturing markets. Personnel in these operations may be more mature themselves, resulting from careers within a developing market company over the years. Maturing markets generate fairly predictable, positive cash flows, and are generally more stable companies. These companies may be ideal training areas for developing managers. Management responsibilities can be high (recall the high cash flow) and management expertise may be exceptional (remember that these operations have proven performers in stock).

3. *Matured markets.* These markets may represent a drain on management time, with their low growth and low returns. As single operating units, little management attention can be devoted to these operations considering their limited profit contribution. From a defensive point of view, the company must manage these operations, but perhaps as a group rather than as individual markets. Grouping matured markets in a single territory may result in reduced operating risks and sufficient management challenge to attract ambitious, well-trained staff. Employees in these operations may be without challenge and extremely frustrated.

4. *Undefined markets.* Such markets have not yet been classified as developing, maturing, or matured. Generally the best personnel available should be assigned to these operations, so that developing and maturing opportunities are not lost. It may be difficult to attract personnel to these operations, unless career incentives are available.

Identifying the subsidiary market classification will help in the proper assignment of personnel and definition of overall organization structure.

Business Characteristics

Each offshore operation may have differing operating characteristics. These should be considered in any staff planning or implementation. For example, a subsidiary with 60 percent of its sales to government agencies should be staffed differently than an operation with only 20 percent government sales.

Channels of distribution may not be the only significant feature that should be analyzed. Consider the concentration of product line sales in each operation as an additional basis for personnel planning. In this section, we will discuss several areas that should be considered in the development of a staffing plan. A manager should not necessarily change his staffing as a result of this analysis, but merely consider each of these areas when he is completing staffing plans.

Primary business activity. Each primary business activity has certain basic requirements. We will not necessarily define all the characteristics of each business, but a brief analysis should stimulate the manager to develop methods of identifying each of the nuances within his specific markets. In Exhibit 6.2, we continue to use the simple requirements definition developed in earlier chapters. The exhibit identifies several types of business activity that may be in effect in each of the subsidiaries.

The requirements definition should be completed at the headquarters, and if possible, be reviewed at the offshore location. The primary headings have been selected as representative of many operations but are not necessarily all-inclusive.

The offshore requirements definition will assist in the development of the worldwide structure. Planners may identify specialty requirements in regions that cannot be supported economically in a specific subsidiary. Shared resources or perhaps consultants should be considered as a means to satisfy this demand. The requirements definition is designed to identify areas of focus. The manager must resolve the resource allocation questions that arise.

Distribution channels. Evaluation of distribution channels should be completed to ensure that appropriate personnel have been hired to properly manage the differing requirements. For example, consider the needs of the business described in Exhibit 6.3. England and Hong Kong may each have $10 million of sales, yet they may have significantly different management and personnel requirements. Note that in the consumer marketing area, substantial financial resources are committed to the marketing effort. This may include marketing, advertising, and sales staff required to coax consumers to purchase the product. This may also be necessary to develop retail awareness ads, so that the product is actively marketed by the retailer.

In the "heavy government" segment, marketing and sales spending is limited, while administrative spending is high. This may be the result of heavy administrative requirements to monitor contract compliance.

Distribution channels should be identified and ranked by their importance to the operation. At a minimum, the following distribution channels should be considered in the analysis of offshore demands: (1) commercial channels (national/international distributors, national wholesaler, retail); (2) government; and (3) original equipment manufacturer.

Definition of product lines. Product lines can impact the offshore unit's staffing levels. Consider the difference between consumer products, medical devices, and complex scientific instruments. Inventory management techniques will vary with each. After the sale, service may have a

Exhibit 6.2
Requirements Definition: Business Activity

	EUROPE				FAR EAST			
	Austria	England	France	Germany	Australia	Japan	Singapore	Taiwan

MANUFACTURING

Engineering Development
   - Product mfg.
   - Design

   Assembly

   Fabrication

DISTRIBUTION

Electronic Product Group
   -Wholesale
   -Retail
   -OEM
   -Distribution - Int'l

Medical Products Group

- Wholesale
- Retail

SERVICE

Warranty repair
Technical Service Agreements

SALES/MARKETING

Advertising development
New product development
Pricing Administration

PROFESSIONAL TRAINING

Technical training
Marketing/advertising training
Sales training

71

Exhibit 6.3
Distribution Channels: Personnel Needs

(000's U.S. $)	England	Hong Kong
Sales		
Government	8,000	2,000
Commercial	2,000	8,000
	10,000	10,000
Gross Profit	5,000	7,000
S. G. & A.		
Marketing	500	1,500
Selling	500	2,000
Gen'l Admin	2,000	1,000
Tech Support	500	500
Total	3,500	5,000
Profit Before Tax	1,500	2,000

significant impact on the selection of personnel. Consider the CAT scan machine, which could be considered a medical device as well as a complex scientific instrument. The staff required to maintain reasonable customer relationships would be scientific, technically trained personnel, not administrative/sales/marketing. The technical aspects of the staff *must* be emphasized. If the primary product line were sunglasses, the emphasis would shift to a more consumer-oriented personality. Heavier merchandising experience would be a necessity.

Product lines may seem to have intuitive characteristics, but the analysis should be completed even though the final answer may appear to be obvious. This analysis will serve as part of the foundation for a long-range plan.

Growth Strategy

After basic business characteristics have been reviewed, it is essential to incorporate them into the long-term strategy. For example, a business may be a maturing market today, but within three years, with the introduction of new products and entry into new markets, management would like the subsidiary to become a developing market. As management reviews long-range plans for the subsidiary, it must concentrate on the strategic plan for the personnel.

Personnel generally represent a long-term, relatively permanent investment. In many countries, the cost of separation is substantial. It is incumbent on the international management to make *strategically developed* personnel decisions. Each of the primary review areas noted above must be considered in relation to the long-range objectives of the business.

Management can significantly influence each area through change in business product line, change in distribution channels, or change in geographic region covered. Through a simple expansion into different countries, perhaps in the "distributor role," the basic character of the business will change. These must be considered in the overall personnel plan to ensure that the strategic objectives of the business plan can be delivered.

Strategic personnel plans should be developed and/or reviewed annually. While this may seem to be excessive review, it should be understood that planning one year in advance is extremely difficult, while three to five years advance planning may be nearly impossible. Redirecting efforts annually to achieve strategic goals is important in any organizational development.

IMPLEMENTING THE ORGANIZATION STRUCTURE

After the initial analyses are completed, it is necessary to define and implement the organization structure. This will consist of a compilation of each of the factors analyzed and balancing staff needs to the organization. This can occur in two ways: (1) by implementing a new organization for a new international operation; or (2) "rationalizing" the existing international organization operations.

Implementing a New Organization

This is the simplest of the organization implementation procedures. Based on a core personnel group (the president, direct reports—e.g., vice president marketing, vice president human resources, etc.), each of the analyses discussed earlier should be considered. A new organization is the ideal time to thoroughly review each of the factors noted. If effective planning and hiring are completed initially, little organizational stress should result in the formative years.

Initial "mistakes" result only from the selection of improper personnel or drastic, unanticipated shifts in the organizational development. A new organization should be reviewed annually to ensure that all developmental factors have been considered. Occasionally, managers disregard the need for an annual review, because the organization has been newly created. The early stages of organization development are as important as a mature organizational review.

Rationalizing the Existing Organization

Rationalization of an organization is the most difficult personnel situation to deal with. The current organization must be thoroughly analyzed and the improved organization must be implemented to ensure the continuing success of the international organization. This could easily result in turmoil in both domestic and offshore operations. This impact must be carefully considered in the planning phase of the rationalization.

Rationalization—that is, a thorough review of the existing personnel—must be completed periodically. Employee capabilities and contribution to the current organization as well as potential future operations must be considered. Individuals with current value in the organization must be carefully developed so that their full potential is realized. Appropriate training courses should be identified and offered to employees to ensure their continued success within the international organization.

Certain positions may be critical to the success of current operations. These positions should be evaluated first, regardless of the potential future implications for individual employees. These positions must be identified as soon as possible to ensure that the international operation maintains a reasonable business status (e.g., a proper return on sales or assets; a reasonable net income). If employees with limited potential are identified, it is necessary to develop alternatives to their careers in international operations.

These circumstances can be resolved through:

1. *Training.* Additional training must be considered an alternative to termination for employees with limited potential. After an employee's training capability is assessed, alternative training courses should be developed to provide the best future for that employee. Although training costs must be considered, these costs must be compared to the possible employee replacement cost. Exhibit 6.4 provides a brief comparison of the alternative costs.

   In addition to the formal training courses available commercially and through local universities, the cost of not training must be evaluated. A simple analysis represents, at best, the subjective judgment of costs. Costs could vary depending on how "employee productivity gaps" are resolved—for example, through use of temporary agency employees or through consultants. These do not, however, consider training cost for new employees or the cost of hiring (e.g., agency fees, relocation).

2. *Promotion.* This may result in immediate promotion for some of the fast-track executives who can deliver desired results immediately. For those considered to

have upward mobility, some additional experience or on-the-job training may be required. Programs should be developed and discussed with these personnel.

Promotions are tangible evidence that the organization is concerned about the employees' welfare. Recall that many of the most promotable individuals may have a reputation for being the most deserving of promotion. These endorsements of the company purpose and concern for the employee are valuable to any rationalization efforts. Many times the individuals who are not worthy of promotion are well known throughout the organization.

3. *Termination.* This is the least desirable alternative. It assumes that an individual cannot provide a service in the international or domestic organizations.

Exhibit 6.4
Cost Analysis: Employee Training

Training costs:

Time on job:

'10 days @ $150 per day	$1,500

Out of pocket:

Tuition	$2,000
Books, supplies, fees	$300

Total	$3,800
	=========

HIRE OUTSIDE REPLACEMENTS

Outplacement costs-

Severance (@ 3 month's)	$9,000
Outplacement training	$2,000
Search fees	$9,000
Relocation	$4,000
On the job training	$4,500

Total	$28,500
	=========

Since this is the least desirable, it is important that decisions be carefully considered. If the decision is taken, it should be implemented quickly, with maximum support to the individual employee. This may include outplacement counseling and full office support during the critical period.

Rationalization is a most difficult process for any existing organization, but occasionally, it must be done. It is critical that all employees recognize that the action is being taken not because of performance but because the organizational needs cannot be satisfied in the future without this action. Personnel should understand that full support has been offered to individuals involved in order to minimize adverse emotions.

Rationalization can also occur through internal counseling. Periodic meetings between the supervisor and the employee could indicate that the employee's future may be limited within the company. Although this does not require termination, the employer is "delivering a message" that should be obvious to the employee. If properly delivered, the employee will search for other opportunities.

After the organization has been implemented and provisions for an annual review have been completed, the company should rely on the managers selected to ensure that the company charter is properly implemented. Further intrusions on the organization should be avoided, provided results meet expectations.

SUMMARY

Throughout this chapter, we have analyzed the current and future needs of the company. The analysis has been a structured approach to organizational analysis. The analysis need not be completed as a one-time effort, but should be completed periodically to ensure the future health of the company. Understanding the company image may be something that is easily understood in the U.S. headquarters, but a completely different image may be projected in offshore units. Management should be aware of this image, and then take the necessary action to ensure that the image is consistent with that desired.

Operating characteristics of the company may be uniform in the U.S. operation, but could vary substantially in offshore markets. Management must again be cognizant of the offshore operating characteristics. These could include varying market profiles, different market positions (developing, maturing, matured, or undefined), product lines offered, distribution channels, and strategic direction.

Organizational plans should be developed based on each of the factors identified. Such plans should be reflected in the training schedules, internal promotions or perhaps outplacement counseling or termination. Each alternative should be carefully considered, because each alternative results in permanent, long-range effects.

CHAPTER 7

INVENTORY MANAGEMENT AND CONTROL

Effective inventory management is essential to all operations, but is especially critical in the international environment. Inventory management in international operations is affected by local customs, elapsed delivery time, tax laws, and perhaps depth of experience in the local management team. This chapter will discuss alternate methods to improve control over inventory investments. In addition, we will discuss product definition, service priority for offshore units, components of inventory costs, and procedures for forecasting and delivering products to offshore affiliates. Simple guidelines will be discussed which can be expanded to individual environments, to ensure that properly defined procedures are implemented.

This chapter will provide a framework in which to analyze the importance of the offshore unit's proper service level, and also analyze inventory by considering several different valuation approaches. The overall objective for inventory is to satisfy customer needs with a minimum inventory risk or cost. Since product sourcing within a country's borders will generally be unaffected by the company's ownership, this will not be discussed. Sourcing from a central location, or the U.S., will be the focus of this chapter, since those situations represent the most significant management challenges.

RESPONSIBILITY FOR INVENTORY CONTROL

In basic terms, the individuals responsible for delivering sales and earnings results *must be responsible* for inventory control. Although this may seem to be an oversimplification, the principle must be the overriding guideline for effective inventory control.

The only purpose to owning inventory is to serve the customer through sales or service.

Review of a brief organization chart and broad definition of responsibilities will illustrate this principle.

Exhibit 7.1 indicates that the general manager is ultimately responsible for inventory control. However, this responsibility must be delegated in order to effectively manage inventory. Major considerations in the delegation of inventory reponsibility are:

1. *Forecasting and ordering.* This responsibility will be limited to the routine forecasting required to maintain adequate stocks of existing products. Strategic forecasting of new or innovative products will not be considered.
2. *Custodial functions.* Physical controls of the inventory are essential to ensure that products reported to be available are actually on hand.
3. *Distribution function.* Effective distribution is critical in international operations, since long lead times and unusual legal/customs regulations must be considered in all distribution.
4. *Reporting.* Report timing in international operations should consider elapsed reporting time and the processing of large orders.

Each of the above functional responsibilities must be considered in a properly designed inventory control system. These functions can be performed by an individual or several departments. Once definite organizational responsibilities have been determined, specific duties can be delegated to staff. Areas to be more thoroughly covered in this chapter will include forecasting/ordering, distribution, and reporting, since the basic custodial function is consistent with a U.S. operation.

STATUS OF OFFSHORE SUBSIDIARY UNIT— SERVICE PRIORITY

If products are sourced from a single location, companies must establish product allocation priorities to ensure equitable service levels to their worldwide customers. Although intercompany activity may occasionally be considered a lower priority for product allocation when compared to current sales in U.S. operations, this may be a serious judgment error if lower priority is the norm. Even if extensive fixed asset investments are not made in a country, a company typically has a high investment in offshore locations. These offshore units represent strategic investments that must be continuously developed through highly qualified technical support and continuous flow of product.

Exhibit 7.1
Organizational Responsibility

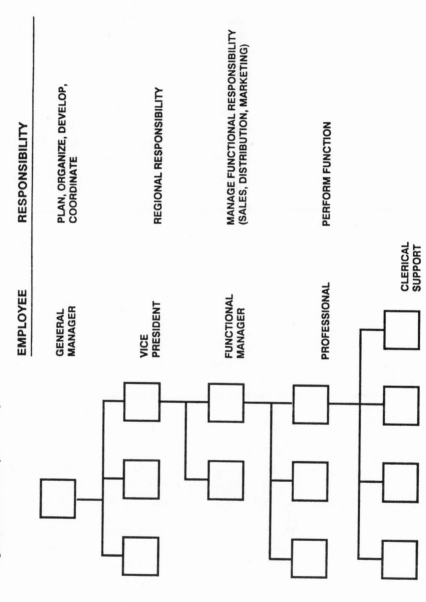

EMPLOYEE	RESPONSIBILITY
GENERAL MANAGER	PLAN, ORGANIZE, DEVELOP, COORDINATE
VICE PRESIDENT	REGIONAL RESPONSIBILITY
FUNCTIONAL MANAGER	MANAGE FUNCTIONAL RESPONSIBILITY (SALES, DISTRIBUTION, MARKETING)
PROFESSIONAL	PERFORM FUNCTION
CLERICAL SUPPORT	

Offshore units may represent the largest individual U.S. customers. As such, they should generally be considered high priority and viewed as preferred customers. Although this should be the established priority, we must consider the skills in each operation, since the units are not necessarily managed consistently. Technical and management skills may vary among subsidiaries. Individual service priorities should be developed based on a review of the operation's ability to manage inventories, and subjective review of strategic importance to the company as a whole. Review points to consider in this analysis should include:

1. *Inventory levels.* The relative measure *Months Inventory on Hand* (MOH) can be used as a basis of comparison to historical levels, other subsidiary's performance, and a theoretical level. This statistic is based on the value of inventory on hand divided by the value of usage over an established period (e.g., many companies use cost of sales over a three-month historical period).

2. *Historical basis—operating characteristics.* This can be monitored through statistics such as reported stock outs, rush orders, or the extent of unusual backorders (items that are generally not in short supply, but appear on the subsidiary backorder lists).

3. *Book-to-physical adjustments.* This is calculated as a percent of average inventory, compared to budget, prior years, and other operations.

4. *Losses due to programmed loss.* This refers to product dating losses and obsolescence losses. Costs should be monitored in relation to prior years, budget, and other subsidiary operations. Each year, expected performance should be budgeted and compared to actual.

5. *Backorder report.* The extent of continuous backorders can be an indicator of inventory management ability. Examples of the review or rating comparisons are included in Exhibit 7.2. These rating factors should be thoroughly reviewed to determine if they are appropriate for a particular operation. Remember, these are performance ratios that can be monitored to improve performance over the years. If specific countries appear to have unusual or deteriorating operating characteristics, graphs of the statistics should be considered.

Service priority is defined to ensure continuous product supply and to understand the quality of offshore management. A twofold program may result from the review: (1) priority service will be established for those with lesser quality operations and high strategic value; (2) increased training for the offshore personnel to improve the quality of management.

In addition to these factors, evaluation of specific marketing strategies could be reflected in the service priorities. For example, the marketing department may require premium service in a specific country to launch a new product or level of customer service, or specifically target efforts against a major competitor. As these decisions are taken, service priorities should change. Service priorities will be conscious management decisions to consider certain countries "top priority" in all processing functions.

Ranking of subsidiaries, using a simple A-B-C approach, from highest priority to lowest priority, would be an effective method of prioritization.

UNDERSTANDING THE COST

Although we must be aware of investment, international costs may differ from U.S. costs, both in size and nature. Four points should be considered in product cost discussion: transfer price, landing costs, sunk costs, and other costs.

Transfer price has been used to describe internal pricing policies. For example, inventory in a country may have an established purchase price from the source, but this may not be the true company cost. Transfer prices represent an internal pricing structure designed to properly distribute income among producing and distributing countries. Transfer prices can affect taxable earnings in many operations, regardless of the actual company cost. An example of transfer pricing follows:

	EXAMPLE 1 Amount	EXAMPLE 2 Amount
Transfer price	75.00	40.00
Manufacturing cost	27.50	27.50
Intercompany profit	47.50	12.50

Intercompany profit must satisfy specific legal and tax regulations, and should be closely reviewed to ensure that proper distribution of profits results. Transfer price methodology should be developed in close coordination with consultants.

If internal profit is not properly considered in the cost analysis, it may distort effective decision making. For example, if landed costs were one of the primary bases for local pricing, company gross profit contribution would be improperly calculated. Contribution for each unit sold, in this example, would be understated by $47.50. Other areas which could be affected by the transfer price decision include make/buy decisions for local production; major marketing programs, considering free product; and inventory control decisions (A-B-C method of risk classification).

Landing costs include additional costs which, in the domestic market, may not be significant. Generally freight, duties, and insurance will be higher in international, when compared to domestic operations. Each of these offshore cost components must be considered in the inventory distribution system. Exhibit 7.3 shows an example of a comparable product analysis.

On a worldwide basis, all product decisions should be made based on the true investment of the company—that is, the $21.20 plus out-of-pocket costs—and worldwide sales. However, individual country market-

Exhibit 7.2
Inventory Review

	M.O.H.			Backorder		
	Act 1987	Bud 1987	Act 1986	Act 1987	Bud 1987	Act 1986
Austria						
Denmark						
England						
France						
Germany						
Italy						
Norway						
Spain						
Sweden						
Switzerland						
Argentina						
Brazil						
Mexico						
Puerto Rico						
Venezuela						
Australia						
Hong Kong						
Japan						
Singapore						
Taiwan						
Total						

ing decisions and product availability decisions in the market should be completed considering the landed cost and intercompany profit. This is true since the company must operate in the local environment. If economic decisions are made based on manufacturing costs only, the required profit contribution to maintain an offshore operation may not be maintained. In effect, the company must maintain an awareness of both the true manufacturing cost and the landed cost to effectively manage an operation.

Sunk cost should be considered in the inventory cost analysis. Sunk costs refer to nonrecoverable investments in inventory (e.g., freight or duties). The country importing the merchandise should review the possibility of duty drawback—that is, a return of the duties paid on imported products —for certain product dispositions. Occasionally "duty drawback" is

Exhibit 7.2 (continued)

	Shrinkage			Shrink %		
	Act 1987	Bud 1987	Act 1986	Act 1987	Bud 1987	Act 1986
Austria						
Denmark						
England						
France						
Germany						
Italy						
Norway						
Spain						
Sweden						
Switzerland						
Argentina						
Brazil						
Mexico						
Puerto Rico						
Venezuela						
Australia						
Hong Kong						
Japan						
Singapore						
Taiwan						
Total						

allowed for specific production disposition, such as local destruction of product, donation to acceptable charitable foundations, or re-export of product to other countries. Before any final product disposition is completed, the company should determine if any drawback is allowed and also define the specific qualifying conditons for drawback. This may reduce "sunk cost."

Freight costs are true "sunk costs"—nonrecoverable except through product sales. Inventory balancing (reallocation of stocks to other operations) must be carefully considered due to the freight investment.

Other costs that are more indirect than those discussed above include obsolescence (both technical and fashion), normal inventory shrinkage, and outdated product. These costs must always be considered before an inventory planning strategy can be defined.

Exhibit 7.3
Landed Cost Analysis

	U.S. Landed Cost	Offshore Landed Cost
Manufacturing cost	$20.00	$20.00
Freight	1.00	2.00
Insurance	.20	.30
Duties	-	2.23
Intercompany Profit		10.00
	---------	----------
Total Cost	21.20	34.53
	=========	===========

DEFINITION OF PRODUCT

Management may consider "inventory" to be a uniform investment. However, a thorough review of inventory can result in classifications that are helpful to management. An annual review of inventory will provide a basis for management to assess existing and future risks, and also to establish broad plans for better management of inventory risks. The following broad classifications have been established to improve management's understanding of inventory investment. Priorities and procedures should vary based on the inventory classification. These classifications represent classical marketing designations and should be considered in any international material control review. Inventory control procedures will vary based on the classifications of inventory identified.

Product life cycle classification is important since timely inventory investment may be critical to a product's continued sale. Three classifications—existing product, new product, and prospective products—are important due to differing inventory control requirements. These designations should be made annually to determine the extent of distribution control required. Designation should be made by the management team to ensure a consistent evaluation and consistently applied controls.

Existing products have a proven usage pattern. Although these patterns may change periodically due to special marketing/sales programs, they will generally follow seasonal patterns. Graphs could be used to effectively control investment in these products. Also, the ratios defined earlier (MOH; book-to-physical adjustment ratios) should be used to monitor effective inventory control. Characteristics of an established product would include few stockouts, few rush orders, and stable MOH, with a low multiple. Controls over these products should be routine and on a predictable timetable (monthly orders, monthly inventory, monthly reporting).

New products require close coordination with the marketing/sales department. Initially, the control ratios (MOH; backorder status; rush orders, etc.) will be different than for an existing product. It is not unusual for new products to have frequent stockouts, rush orders, and extremely high MOH when compared to existing products. Close review of investments in new products is critical to their success. Remember, if the products are not available for distribution in the market, they cannot be sold.

Controls over these products should reflect their volatile nature. Frequent ad hoc reporting in addition to monthy reporting is essential to maintain the proper level of material management.

Prospective products are those not yet introduced, but in a preproduction phase. These products represent the most risk in the international arena, since they may not have been previously classified for import. Remember, each product must be properly declared before import. Products must be carefully reviewed to ensure the best form of import declaration, since a proper declaration may result in lower duties and also reduced clearing efforts in the future. In addition to importation regulations, other government regulations and registrations may be required before introduction in the market.

Controls over these products are primarily administrative or legal, designed to effectively guarantee smooth, minimum cost importation.

All inventories can be easily classified by their values, either current inventory levels or flow through usage. This is the A-B-C method of inventory classification. This simple principle requires that all inventories be reviewed in a high-low listing, to determine the highest concentration of investment or the products with the greatest cumulative total cost for the year.

If we were to review the existing inventory, a high-low listing would help to focus management attention on the most critical items in stock.

A items are the most valuable, based on annual usage. These items generally represent few stock keeping units (SKUs), but a major portion of the inventory investment during the year. The *A* classification should be based on those items which cumulatively represent the most valuable 15 to 20 percent of units of the population. *B* items are the second tier of investment, and represent about the next 20 to 30 percent of units in the high-low inventory report. This segment will represent more items or SKUs of inventory. C items are all remaining items.,

Exhibit 7.4 shows that through sorting by value to the company, management attention to the top 20 percent of products may reduce overall inventory risk. Exhibit 7.4 also indicates the value of the A-B-C method of classification. Note that the high dollar value items are only about 15 percent of the SKUs represented. Management control systems should be developed to ensure close control over A and B items. Less rigorous review and reporting will be required for C items.

Marketing designation represents items identified by the marketing/sales departments as critical inventory items. Special attention should be devoted to such items, since major investments in promotion and advertising may be planned. Advance preparation for the inventory demand should be identified by the marketing department, and should be completed well in advance of the time needed, to ensure that products are available for distribution.

ORDERING/FORECASTING PROCEDURES

After inventory carryng costs are understood and the overall service strategy developed, the product must be made available to supply customer demand. Forecasting must consider all of the previously mentioned factors, and also lead times, forecasting content, format, and frequency. Specific planning criteria must be established and coordinated with domestic divisions in order to ensure that proper supply levels are available. The major time factors are depicted in Exhibit 7.5. Each of the factors must be considered in the development of forecasts or order procedures and timetables. Forecast timing or order processing must consider the lead time to complete the order/shipping process.

Order Preparation

Order preparation should be a simple, routine procedure. In fact, many times order preparation and approval may be delegated to a low organizational level due to the simple ordering format. However, a thorough analysis of each order is crucial to the continued customer service effort. Exhibit 7.6 is an example of the support that should be available for review of an order. Note that the form includes an approval section and several sections for management review. Comparative statistics such as prior month's usage, three-months prior usage, and the current forecast for the period (updated several times during the current year). This reference data has been included to provide a complete basis for review.

Exhibit 7.4
A-B-C Classification

Description	Prod Number	Invent Units	Unit Value	Extended Value	% of Total
Chip - Micro circ	10395	1,424	19.44	27,682.56	18.29%
Chip - Micro circ	10320	1,332	14.79	19,700.28	13.02%
Wire - Cop 6 ga	10230	4,566	4.24	19,359.84	12.79%
Wire - Cop 8 ga	10245	4,288	3.97	17,023.36	11.25%
Wire - Gold 6 ga	10215	646	22.79	14,722.34	9.73%
Chip - Micro circ	10380	767	17.47	13,399.49	8.85%
Chip - Micro circ	10365	498	26.00	12,948.00	8.56%
Chip - Micro circ	10350	466	19.88	9,264.08	6.12%
Wire - Gold 10 ga	10185	567	13.57	7,694.19	5.08%
Wire - Gold 12 ga	10155	354	12.47	4,414.38	2.92%
Clip - 80 mm	10140	3,333	0.40	1,333.20	0.88%
Chip - Micro circ	10335	42	27.77	1,166.34	0.77%
Wire - Gold 8 ga	10170	44	16.77	737.88	0.49%
Wire - Gold 14 ga	10200	55	9.77	537.35	0.36%
Chip - Micro circ	10305	24	13.27	318.48	0.21%
Wire - Cop 10 ga	10260	76	3.75	285.00	0.19%
Wire - Cop 12 ga	10275	77	3.34	257.18	0.17%
Clip - 60 mm	10110	678	0.35	237.30	0.16%
Clip - 70 mm	10125	456	0.35	159.60	0.11%
Clip - 30 mm	10065	277	0.12	33.24	0.02%
Clip - 20 mm	10050	300	0.10	30.00	0.02%
Wire - Cop 14 ga	10290	5	2.97	14.85	0.01%
Clip - 50 mm	10095	44	0.22	9.68	0.01%
Clip - 40 mm	10080	23	0.15	3.45	0.00%
Total				151,332.07	1.00

Each of the factors must be considered to ensure adequate supply. Format or means of preparation may vary among companies but each factor represents a point of risk analysis.

Although companies may allow the materials control group exclusively to prepare the forecast/order, this may not provide full insight into the marketing program. Forecasts should be endorsed by all key members of the offshore management team (marketing, sales, materials control, and general management). The endorsement does not require examination of all the details, but rather a confirmation of the underlying assumptions for preparation. Remember, the order may be the only supply link during the next 30/60 days. Out-of-stock conditions may result in missed objectives.

Monthly orders should be standardized. A monthly order should include a brief narrative describing any significant features about the current inventory position, possible exposures, or windfalls expected in

Exhibit 7.5
Order Processing Timetable

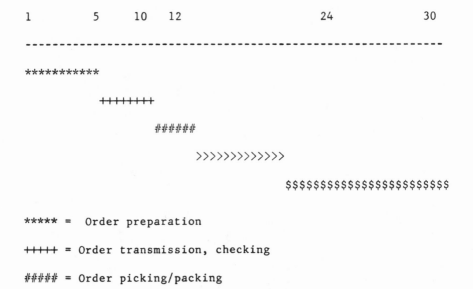

```
1          5     10   12                           24                   30

-------------------------------------------------------------------

***********

            ++++++++

                  ######

                     >>>>>>>>>>>>>

                                $$$$$$$$$$$$$$$$$$$$$$$$$$$$$$

***** =  Order preparation

+++++ = Order transmission, checking

##### = Order picking/packing

>>>>> = Order shipping, transit time

$$$$$ = Order clearing, unpacking, warehousing
```

the future. Exhibit 7.7 provides an example of a completed order, including the necessary approvals, appropriate graphics, and a narrative describing essential information.

Shipping/Order Transit

Each of the time factors must be considered in the forecasting process. Note that the greatest time constraint is shipping and customs clearing. Firm order processing timetables should be established. In order to avoid critical rush periods, the source company should consider the impact of the large restocking orders and attempt to smooth the order cycle through a thorough analysis of order flow and close coordination of the order process.

Each of the factors noted should be thoroughly reviewed to determine the appropriate order processing time. For example, the first two phases of the processing cycle—order preparation and transmission—should be fairly simple and consistent among all international subsidiaries.

Exhibit 7.6
Order Form

Date: _____

```
-----------------------------------------------------------------------
                                                     **
Prod Descrip      Product    Inventory     Usa age    Quarter  **  Order
                  Number                ------------------Forecast **  Quantity
                             Month      3 Months             **
                                                            **
=================================================================**  =========
                                                            **
                                                            **
                                                            **
```

```
                                                   **
                                                   **
                                                   **
                                                   **
                                                   **
                                                   **
                                                   **
                                                   **
                                                   **
                                                   **
                                                   **
                                                   **
                                                   **
                                                   **
                                                   **
                                                   **
                                                   **
                                                   **
                                                   **
                                                   **
                                                   **
                                                   **
```

Prepared By:

Reviewed By:

Approved By:

Exhibit 7.7
Sample Order

Prod Descrip	Product Number	Inventory	Usa age Month	3 Months	Quarter Forecast	**	Order Quantity
Chip - Micro circ	10395	200	177	427	700	**	300
Chip - Micro circ	10320	122	25	57	100	**	0
Chip - Micro circ	10350	135	47	208	350	**	300
Chip - Micro circ	10305	22	12	0	0	**	0

Prepared By:

Reviewed By:

Approved By:

However, the shipping lead time and customs clearing time may vary substantially by subsidiary (see Exhibit 7.8).

Note that the total delivery time varies by subsidiary, based on the shipping transit time and the customs clearing time. These components should be reviewed periodically to ensure that major changes in expected delivery are properly accommodated. Generally, inventories should be reviewed and orders processed at least monthly. Transit time can be monitored by periodically checking the broker performance during the year. Random shipments should be selected and the time to complete the order/shipment cycle should be monitored. Transit time can be modified through premium transit (airfreight, or courier) and should be considered when developing the overall service level required.

Exhibit 7.8
Comparative Shipping Clearing Time

```
                                  DAYS ELAPSED

          1                       10                      20
          _____

Canada    *******++++

Mexico        ******************++++++++++++++++++++++++++++++++++++++

France    *****************+++++++++++++

Australia    **********************************+++++++
```

****** = Shipping time

++++++ = Customs clearing

Customs clearing time may be affected by the selection of the local broker. Larger, better-established brokers may have well-defined systems and administrative staff to properly clear shipments. Also, experienced brokers may provide additional insight into the best form of customs declaration, thereby reducing duties or improving customs clearing time. A close alliance with a quality broker may also improve the customs declaration and clearing process for new product introductions.

For example, a computer manufacturer may import partially assembled computers for assembly. If the import is declared as computer parts, duties may be assessed at a 75 percent rate. If, through review of the customs regulations, it is determined that a proper declaration could be made as "electrical components—parts for assembly," duties may be reduced to 20 percent. This information could be available through a high quality broker.

Order Control Procedures

Effective order control is important in international operations due to the high cost of stock-out for a subsidiary operation and long lead times for shipping and clearing. The entire investment—the entire equity of the offshore operation—rests on proper customer service. The international subsidiary may be the single largest customer of the U.S. corporation.

International orders should be closely controlled through order processing logs and established processing timetables.

Each order should include an acknowledgment, indicating order status, expected completion date, and a log reference number. While this may appear to be an administrative burden, recall that these operations represent the most important customers. Monthly control reports should be prepared for materials management indicating service levels and any problems encountered. All order correspondence should be maintained in separate files, so that each order can be effectively monitored. An example of a simple control is the log illustrated in Exhibit 7.9.

Forecasting

Forecasting techniques can range from simple trend analysis to sophisticated scientific regression methods. Trend analysis should be completed for major products or product groups.

Monthly trend analysis may provide an uneven chart that is difficult to interpret. Long-range patterns or seasonal effects may be evident upon closer review.

Moving average trend analysis will provide a better idea of any operating cycle or other meaningful patterns. For example, if weekly sales trends were being reviewed, a four-week moving average may be useful to monitor trends. Four weeks could represent a monthly cycle. Exhibit 7.10 shows weekly sales and a four-week moving average.

Regression analysis is a statistical method that can be used to predict future trends or usage. Regression analysis projects probabilities, based on a correlation with certain independent variables. Regression analysis can be used in time series, or with other products or events that can be monitored. Regression formulas are available in many production or operations management texts, or software packages can be used to develop applications for specific operations.

Regardless of the method chosen to develop forecasts, management judgment is a key variable in all forecasting. Future decisions that cannot necessarily be quantified and entered into a regression formula or chart must be reflected in all forecasts. Management teams are responsible for forecasts, not mathematical formulas.

OTHER CRITICAL FACTORS

Thus far we have reviewed forecast techniques, order processing procedures, and shipping/clearing/timing. We have discussed the required monthly inventory report, which should include a brief narrative describing any issues considered important by the offshore operations.

Exhibit 7.9
Order Control Log

Order Control Number	Date Rec'd	Acknowl Sent	Country	Products			Status			
				Mech	Elec	Micro	Complete	Partial	Partial	Partial

Exhibit 7.10
Weekly Sales Chart

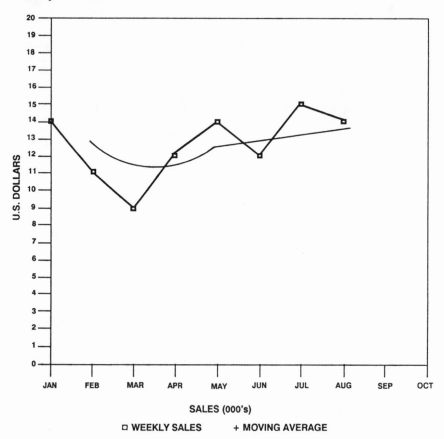

SALES (000's)

□ WEEKLY SALES   + MOVING AVERAGE

However, we must emphasize that these offshore operations represent major customers. Just as any effective operation must constantly monitor the customer's perceptions of the company, the materials management must continually monitor the effectiveness of the organization. Frequent informal contact should be made to ensure that the procedures are effective.

The monthly narrative can be used as a method to inform all subsidiaries of potential benefits/problems within their inventories. Although it must be clear that responsibility for effective control of the inventory remains with the offshore units, occasional support to more effectively balance their inventories may be appropriate. If serious out-of-balance inventory conditions are identified, a closely coordinated, properly developed program to reduce this imbalance may be appropriate.

Such programs should be considered in a monthly report to U.S. management. Recall that the decision pyramid requires that appropriate information be transmitted to appropriate management levels.

SUMMARY

Inventory generally represents a major investment for all operations. Through diligent use of simple management techniques, investments can be minimized and operating risks can be reduced. Planning investment and control procedures before the investment is made and a thorough review of the investments using several different techniques will help management gain additional insight into the operation.

International inventory control can provide excellent rewards, but without proper controls can result in serious profit drains. Management must thoroughly prepare for the international market by defining appropriate control statistics and monitoring subsidiary performance on a routine basis. This chapter presents certain review techniques which, if used, would result in effective inventory control. Through effective hiring practices and proper monitoring, each offshore operation will be successful.

CHAPTER 8

CASH CONTROL:
AN AWARENESS

How many times have we considered "money in the bank" to be the most secure? Compare money in the bank to real estate (not very liquid), stocks (such volatility belongs to risk takers), or perhaps tangible assets such as machinery and equipment (not very marketable). In international operations, cash may also be the best of all worlds, or perhaps have the attributes of some of the other assets described. It is important to understand that in the United States, we live in a "world of our own." We can travel coast to coast or travel to a major island chain in the Pacific and always use the same U.S. currency. It is always valued at $1.00—never a liquidity problem. It is easy to spend anywhere within U.S. borders.

In addition, the U.S. dollar tends to be a universally acceptable "world" currency. For major transactions and routine touring, the U.S. dollar can be used successfully in trade. Unfortunately, the U.S. dollar cannot be used as the basic currency for all transactions. Each country has a national currency, related to other worldwide currencies, based on economic and political factors. This chapter will delve further into the volatility of worldwide currencies as they relate to effective business management and risk analysis and control.

The reader should understand that *cash* can mean today's balances deposited in the bank or perhaps commitments to pay value in the future. Each of these circumstances has risk and opportunity associated with the actions taken in the world market.

This chapter will discuss some of the risk and opportunities in cash management, and various methods to minimize or control these risks. Simple examples will be used to demonstrate salient points. One of the most essential actions to be taken by management is to establish good working relationships with bankers to enlist their support and use their expertise.

RISKS IN CASH MANAGEMENT

Cash management in international operations has risks, simply because the U.S. dollar is not necessarily the currency used. Foreign governments and their economies will affect the overall relationship of their currency to the U.S. dollar. Companies must be conscious of all offshore investments, which can range from an account receivable due in a foreign currency to a major investment, such as a subsidiary operation. Foreign government actions can affect the valuation of these assets.

Revaluation/Devaluation

Currency relationships among countries have been the subject of review by scholars for years. Perfect correlation among currencies does not exist over the short term. However, currencies, over the long term, will vary based on the relationships of inflation and interest rates. We will not discuss the way currencies interact, but instead will review the end products of those interactions.

Currency devaluations affect company assets, because the asset values have been realigned to a world standard. Investment offshore carries certain risks that must be understood. Currency rates and relationships change, because this is an ever changing world. As the rates change, company values change. Note in Exhibit 8.1 that the value of the cash in U.S. dollar terms continuously deteriorates as the currency devalues. If a company had invested the 10 million cruzeiros in a U.S. dollar account, the value in U.S. dollars would not deteriorate from the initial deposit of $500,000.

Companies can protect themselves from these foreign exchange effects through implementation of a well-developed cash plan. Note in Exhibit 8.1 that liabilities have also been affected by the devaluation. The value of the liabilities has declined from $100,000 to $60,000. One may conclude from this brief example that the best financial position is that of a net debtor in countries with devaluations. This may be an inaccurate conclusion, since, with major devaluations, interest rates are also extreme.

Recent examples in Latin American countries include Brazil, Argentina (where new currencies were initiated after years of serious devaluations and economic chaos), and Mexico. In each of these countries, hyperinflation and excessive interest have been the norm. Inflation rates of up to 500 percent annually have been the norm. Inflation rates of up to 500 percent annually have been experienced in these countries. Extremely high interest rates accompany high inflation. Interest in these countries has been in

Exhibit 8.1
Revaluation/Devaluation

(000's)

	Local Currency	Rate @ .5/$	Rate @ .7/$
Cash	1000	500	700
Accounts Receivable	5000	2500	3500
Inventory	5000	2500	3500
Prepaid Assets	500	250	350
Fixed Assets - Net	2000	1000	1400
Total Assets	13500	6750	9450
Accounts Payable	1000	500	700
*Accrued Liabilities	1000	500	700
Long Term Debt - Current	500	250	350
Long Term Debt	8000	4000	5600
Equity	3000	1500	2100
Total Liab/Equity	13500	6750	9450

excess of 500 percent. Exhibit 8.2 demonstrates the effects of hyperinflation. Note that the accumulated interest exceeds the initial principal in
only four months.

The example, although exaggerated, also illustrates the effects of
devaluations on a local currency. Countries with significant devaluations
generally have very high inflation and interest rates. Note that although
the principal plus interest has grown to 2,986,000 cr., the U.S. dollar
value remains at about $210,000.

Devaluations and revaluations can seriously affect reported results and
invested equity. All managers should be wary of these effects when considering offshore activity (not just offshore subsidiaries, but also assets and
liabilities denominated in a foreign currency). Cash plans should reflect
current projections of foreign exchange movement.

Established Currency Restrictions

In addition to the somewhat random effects of currency variance, governments or federal reserve banks may restrict cash movement for predetermined transactions (e.g., sale of merchandise). Several circumstances

Exhibit 8.2
Example: Hyperinflation

(000's $)	P E R I O D					
	1	2	3	4	5	6
Debt	1,000	1,200	1,440	1,728	2,074	2,488
Interest @20%	1,200	1,440	1,728	2,074	2,488	2,986

where government policy may directly affect cash management are: dividend policy, import/export licensing for merchandise, and technology licensing. For example, in the case of initial investments in an operation, the government may restrict cash dividends paid out. In some countries, minimum retained earnings balances are required before any dividends are declared or paid.

In certain sales or purchasing activities, preliminary approval for cash transfer is required. This is generally thoroughly defined in import/export license requirements. Central banks may coordinate transfer of funds after a thorough review of export/import documents, license agreements, proof of delivery, and so on. Central banks may also delay remittances to establish a currency float. This generally occurs in closely controlled economies with limited hard currency reserves (e.g., many Latin American and some Far Eastern countries restrict hard currency flow).

Frozen Assets—Government Action

During 1987 the government of Brazil blocked all hard currency loan repayments. In effect, the government unilaterally decided to discontinue all of the U.S. dollar or hard currency outflow, except for critical import items. This has occurred in many countries during the past fifteen years (Mexico, Iran, China, Bolivia, Peru, etc.).

Based on government directive, a country's central banks discontinue cash availability. Business investors must understand the risks in each country. International banks and information services are available to rank the risks of various countries. *Business International Money Report*, published by the Business International Corporation, provides an excellent overall analysis of country risk. Weekly reports are prepared, covering specific news issues, and country risks are evaluated annually.

If a government elects to freeze hard currency assets, there are few alternatives to correct the situation. Currency swaps or futures may be an alternative, but should be carefully considered due to potential risks. In any hedging activity, it is essential that all governmental regulations have been considered.

OTHER CONSIDERATIONS

Liquidity of Currency

Development of a cash strategy using all the elements of typical treasury management must consider the depth of the currency market. Market depth relates to the amount of currency traded. If substantial quantities are traded, the market has "depth." If currency hedges are considered essential due to identified currency risk, futures may not be available to cover the risks. As cash strategies are developed, the company must consider the depth of the markets. Irish pounds, for example, are not traded as frequently as German marks or Japanese yen.

A brief example of "depth" is as follow:

	British Pounds	German Marks	Japanese Yen	Irish Pounds
Annual transactions (billions $)	$50	$100	$800	$10

If we were interested in investing in a foreign currency, it would be much easier to find buyers and sellers of yen, compared to Irish pounds.

Currency liquidity is an important consideration in cash strategy

---

Strategy may be well defined, but due to the depth of the market, it may be impossible to implement.

Accounting for Cash and Strategy

Despite the fact that a well-defined strategy may be in place, and the depth of the market is sufficient to accommodate that strategy, all the efforts may be in vain if the proper accounting regulations have not been followed. Recall that FASB 52 describes the proper accounting protocol for foreign currency effects. Cash management has been considered within the bounds of the statement. If proper management actions are not taken and documented at certain critical times, the desired hedging or cash management strategy cannot be recorded as expected. Some examples of accounting regulations that must be closely adhered to include:

1. *Hedge against existing payable.* Fixed foreign exchange commitments may exist for future payment. Foreign exchange forwards or other hedges may be employed to offset or balance the effects of foreign exchange fluctuations. If hedges are taken for specific liabilities, appropriate levels of management must declare the purpose to properly account for the transaction.

2. *Hedges against potential future commitment.* Hedges may be established for future transactions (e.g., if all sales are foreign-sourced product, a minimum hedge may be established for expected future purchases). If such hedging is completed, the hedge must be properly identified to ensure the proper accounting result.

3. *Hedge against long-term debt or equity investment.* In order to protect against the effects of currency fluctuations on long-term debt or basic equity value, a

company may choose to hedge these values. Again, management must properly assign the hedge against the values to ensure that the proper accounting is completed.

Management decisions should closely involve key business managers, including accounting, treasury, and tax. Without full involvement, results may be different than expected. Close coordination with someone familiar with FASB 52 is essential for proper results.

Tax Considerations

Tax laws can severely affect cash management strategy. Consider the effects of the most recent legislation changing the tax impact of long-term capital gain/loss. In addition to the change in captial gains, consider the impact of timing of tax payments. As cash management strategies are defined, a selection of alternatives should be developed and evaluated by the management team. Each alternative should be carefully evaluated considering the tax implications.

RISK AVOIDANCE STRATEGY

Risk can be minimized through effective cash controls. As with any business transaction, careful planning and control as well as definition of purpose are important. Proper definition of routine reporting is essential to proper cash control. This reporting can be internal or through outside services (e.g., the banks involved).

Strategies must be well developed, considering the business objectives. Many multinationals are satisfied to merely protect earned profits. This strategy assumes that the company is best at developing, manufacturing, and distributing product, but is not in the business of forecasting and maximizing gains in foreign exchange. This strategy is generally considered a defensive one.

Aggressive strategies define a "profit motive" for their foreign exchange activity. Some companies consider the treasury function to be staffed by professionals who understand their trade well enough to allow modest, well-controlled ventures into aggressive foreign currency management.

In either case, company management wants to obtain the maximum benefit from the foreign exchange strategy selected. If improper controls and techniques are employed, risks may increase, and losses or opportunity costs may result.

Cash Reporting

Since cash could be an extremely volatile commodity, it is important to have timely reporting. Cash reporting can be completed using internal systems or banking systems. Either method requires prompt, accurate information about cash balances, overdraft positions, other liabilities, and currency. In chapter 3 we discussed simple reporting for cash. More in-depth reporting is described in Exhibit 8.3. Note such factors as interest rate, currency of record, bank, and other related restrictions. This information is important to review, to ensure that worldwide currency exposures have been considered in monthly transactions.

In a multiple facility company, intercompany transactions occur frequently and may actually be offsetting within the system. In these situations, a worldwide netting system could reduce overall exposures and transaction costs in the hedging and settlement process. It should be noted that currency regulations governing international monetary settlements must be carefully considered in any netting system. Banks may be an ideal source of information for these regulations. Netting will, at a minimum, reduce transaction fees and could potentially be a means to centralize all foreign exchange reporting. Reporting frequency and content should be determined on a case-by-case basis, considering many factors.

Foreign Exchange Contracts

In addition to cash reporting, all foreign exchange (FX) contracts should be summarized monthly and should be confirmed by management at least annually. FX contract summaries should include transaction rates, contract duration, and settlement dates; they should be designated "hedge," to ensure proper accounting treatment. Major contracts should require countersignature (approval) by a corporate officer.

Foreign exchange is an extremely volatile area that is highly leveraged. Due to the generally weaker controls than in cash and the extremely high leverage of foreign exchange contracts, extreme caution should be exercised in this area.

Banking Relationships

There is no doubt that banks earn money by providing service to customers. These services include foreign exchange forecasts, assistance in the development of cash strategy, and development of banking systems that can minimize cash or foreign exchange risk. It is important to establish a good working relationship with an international bank with subsidiaries or associate banks in foreign locations. Selection of a bank can be completed by understanding company needs and identifying banks nearby that can provide the required service.

Exhibit 8.3
Cash Reporting

Country Code: Japan

ASSETS

	CURRENCY CODE	BANK	INTEREST RATE	RESTRICTIONS	VALUE	NOTES
Irish Pounds	A	Chase Manhattan	4.50	90 day term	10,000	
German DM	B	Deutsche Bank	4.00	6 mo Cert Dep	1,000	
Japan Yen	C	Sumitomo	4.25	Demand	1,040,000	
U.S. $	D	Manuf's Han	5.00	Demand	5,000	

LIABILITIES

Accounts Payable	Currency code	Payee	Interest Rate	Due Date	Amount Due	Notes
U.S. $	D	Various		April 30	4,000	Collateralized by A/R
Japanese yen	C	Sumitomo	7.50	April 7	25,000	
German DM	B	Chase Manhattan	7.00	April 15	1,000	

Cash Flow Forecasting

Cash flow forecasting is the heart of any risk avoidance and control system. Cash flow forecasting should include both short- and long-term forecasts.

Short-term forecasts. Short-term forecasts can range anywhere from three months to one to three years. It is difficult to forecast beyond three years due to the ever changing legal and economic environment. However, short-term forecasts should be prepared throughout the year, and periodic annual forecasts should be developed. Exhibit 8.4 demonstrates one form of forecast that could be useful. Note that the forecast is segmented into intercompany, bank, and other. This information will be useful in overall planning.

Long-term forecasts. Long-term forecasts are important since most offshore operations are considered permanent investments. Cash planning, such as future dividend payments or reinvestment in facilities for expansion, must be considered in initial planning. In addition, such long-term factors as debt financing and repayment plans must be developed in the long-range plan. For example, consider the options for financing a major offshore acquisition.

Acquisitions may provide adequate cash flow to service the acquisition debt, and perhaps should be financed in a local currency. This approach would match risks of the foreign currency to the borrowing, reducing overall foreign exchange exposure.

In addition to acquisitions, dividend policy and internal investments and expansion must be considered in the long-range plans. Can you imagine having millions of dollars invested in a foreign operation, but not be able to use the money for additional investment? This can occur without adequate strategic planning.

Long-range cash flow policies must be developed in close cooperation with the operations management teams. Their operations will either use or generate cash that must be protected from risk and also properly invested to provide maximum returns to stockholders.

RISK ALTERNATIVES

Thus far we have discussed cash planning and risk assessment through discussions with bankers and independent agencies. We have also developed several reports that can be used to monitor cash flow and control day-to-day risks. After we have identified the risks and opportunities, what can we do to minimize these potential costs? Alternatives to established cash management risks can take many forms. We will concentrate

Exhibit 8.4
Short-Term Cash Needs

Country: Germany

Currency: U.S. $ Equivalent

	Record Currency	Jan	Feb	Mar	Apr	May	June
Intercompany							

Japan	Yen	25	20	30	40	20	30
Hong Kong		10	10	10	10	10	10
Australia		5	5	5	5	5	5
Subtotal		40	35	45	55	35	45
Bank							

Chase	DM	-27	-20	-20	-20	-25	-27
Manufacturer's Hanover	U.S. $	-10	-10	-10	-10	-10	-10
Subtotal		-37	-30	-30	-30	-35	-37
Other							

A/P		-20	-20	5	-3	-5	-6
Total Cash Forecast		-17	-15	20	22	-5	2

on four primary tools to minimize risk: forwards, or forward contracts, futures, swaps, and options. We will highlight each type of tool and also describe methods and timing for their use.

Forwards

Forwards are simply agreements between two individuals to exchange a certain value of foreign currency at a predetermined exchange rate and at an established time. Although many people believe that a forward rate defines the direction of currency movement, when compared to the existing "spot" rate, this is not necessarily true. The difference between a forward rate and the existing spot rate is the interest value of money.

If two parties know the prevailing spot rate and agree to exchange currencies at a future date at another valuation level, the arbitrage market requires that the only difference between the rates be the interest value of investments in the two currencies. Forwards can be used successfully to guarantee certain levels of exchange in the future. For example, if a business had purchase commitments in one year for 100 million yen, and the yen was expected to increase in value, a company may buy "forward" to ensure a constant cost of product. Companies with large expected inflows of foreign exchange may sell forward to ensure that specific levels of profit are locked-in in markets with expected declines in currency value.

Forwards are products of major financial institutions and have short terms (from three to twelve months). As such, forwards are generally used for short-term hedges, although it is possible to "roll over" the contracts end-to-end to maintain long-term coverage. Such a policy of rollovers may cover foreign exchange risk, but may require substantially more administrative effort and risk than some other alternatives.

Futures

Futures are institutionalized forwards. Futures are publicly traded on exchanges and are highly "liquid" compared to forwards. Futures trading through brokerage houses involves little credit risk, since daily cash "balancing" is done. Exposures created through futures trading must be settled daily, thereby reducing any credit risk that may be present with a "forward" contract. Maximum loss would be one day's fluctuation, rather than the full term.

Futures are traded in preestablished values, for routinely specified terms. Futures are ideal methods for avoiding foreign currency risk, since they are for short terms (e.g., up to one year) and remain highly liquid, since they are traded on established exchanges.

Swaps

Swaps are individually negotiated "trades" of debt of one currency for another, at the time of the swap contract. Exchange rates used to value the swap are the spot rates prevailing at the time of the transaction. Swaps are not traded on the exchanges, and are generally coordinated through financial institutions.

Due to the negotiation requirement, swaps are generally for longer term debt/cash structuring. For example, a swap is an ideal method for financing a foreign acquisition. Company A, which wants to buy company C for $100 million of British pounds, may negotiate with a financial institution to develop an alternative investor. Company B may wish to invest $100 million of British pounds in a U.S. company. Neither company wants to be subject to currency variance. Since each local acquisition will generate sufficient cash to pay off the entire debt within approximately the same number of years, a swap is organized. That is, company A exchanges $100 million of dollars for British pounds today, and both companies agree to exchange the same number of units of currency in the future.

However, since there may be a real value differential between the two currencies due to the difference in interest rates, periodic remittances between the companies may be required to compensate for the difference in interest rates.

Options

An option differs from each of the above instruments, since it is an agreement with the right to buy or the right to sell currencies at specified rates, at specified times. Options generally have a life of less than one year, and are traded on exchanges. An option does not require final consummation. For example, if the buyer of a "put" (the right to sell currency at a specified price) finds that the present value of the currency is greater than his right to sell, he will simply allow his option to expire. All other instruments described must be completed at the expiration of the term. For example, if the company had a 90-day futures contract, at the end of 90 days there must be a settlement of the contract.

Option buyers have limited risk (loss of premium) and significant upside potential (limited only by the market movement).

SUMMARY

Throughout this chapter, cash management and foreign exchange risks and opportunities have been discussed. As with all other situations in business, a thorough analysis of the risks and development of a selection of alternatives by business professionals should result in a controlled or minimum risk environment. Cash management is similar to effective inventory control, since we are dealing with a potentially volatile asset with immediate liquidity, and a significant potential for loss if mismanaged. Specialized tools for "cash and risk management" have been developed, which if properly implemented will maximize returns. Unfortunately, some of the tools represent highly leveraged, lesser controlled means to minimize risk. As such, effective internal control and periodic management confirmation must be completed. Overall, these tools will reduce operation risks if properly managed by a team of trained specialists.

CHAPTER 9

PLANNING ACQUISITIONS AND INTERNATIONAL EXPANSION

In the past, Wall Street has developed a frenzied pace of company acquisitions and industry consolidations. These activities have resulted from extensive analysis concentrating on financial operating ratios and perceived business synergies. This chapter will provide a basis for an analytical review of business activity that should occur during and immediately after the purchase transaction occurs. Although the chapter should help management develop a plan for successful integration of an acquired company into ongoing operations, it is not a "cookbook" to be followed in a step-by-step fashion to a successful integration. Management judgment is subjective and yet essential to properly assess acquisition motives and develop appropriate integration plans.

Sections of this chapter may be reviewed several times to more thoroughly understand the motives for acquisition and the transition plans required.

The chapter has three main emphases: (1) review of the buyer's logic to acquire a business; (2) developing integration plans based on the reason for acquisition; and (3) developing the international operation through distributors. Throughout the chapter, risk analysis graphs will be included to focus the reader's attention on the major risks in each type of expansion.

MOTIVATION—REASONS FOR EXPANSION

Basic reasons for expansion can range from pure emotion (for an unsophisticated entrepreneur) to sound business reasons, such as product line or geographic expansion. It is not essential to list all the reasons for acquiring a business, but the basic motivation should be understood, since understanding the motive will provide the foundation for an integration plan.

Selected business expansion motives will be reviewed, but these represent only a few explanations for business expansion. The focal point of the chapter will be the management activity necessary to achieve business deliverables, assess personnel needs, and complete an overall organization review. Acquisition rationale reviewed will be limited to such factors as: expanded product line, vertical product integration, geographic expansion, and new strategic direction.

Motivation in acquisitions must be understood, since negotiations will be affected. In all negotiations, it is essential to define negotiation parameters within the company and then to stay within these parameters. Maximum purchase price, alternative methods of payment, liabilities assumed, and so on must be defined in the initial buying strategy, and the conditions must be adhered to.

Expanded Product Line

Product line expansion can occur through purchase of specific products from a company or acquisition of an entire company. Although the acquisition may be a very expensive method of expanding current operations, there may be immediate, high returns.

The additional product line should be thoroughly reviewed to identify duplicate lines. For example, a new product line, while not an exact substitute for an existing line, may cannibalize some of the exisitng sales. A thorough marketing review should be completed. If duplication exists, complete transition plans should be developed to ensure that the impact on existing operations has been properly considered.

Furthermore, training requirements should be thoroughly evaluated. Although product lines may be similar, additional sales force technical training may be required.

Finally, manufacturing and distribution requirements must be assessed to ensure compatibility. The manufacture of expanded product lines may require substantially different capital equipment or management resources. Careful review by manufacturing experts will ensure continued success with a minimum disruption. Exhibit 9.1 provides an example of several common points to be reviewed in a product line analysis. Separate plans should be developed to understand optimistic/pessimistic and most likely scenarios. Each "incremental impact" should be thoroughly analyzed and rough plans to deliver should be prepared.

The distribution implications are critical to ensure that the new product line fulfills expectations while maintaining service in existing lines. Manufacturing may require additional support services not yet available in operations. In each of these circumstances, specific transition plans should be prepared. A careful review of future manufacturing and distribution considerations should be completed with responsible management. Customer service risks are minimized during a product line expansion, since established distribution channels are used (see Exhibit 9.2).

Expanded Geographical Market

Broader distribution of existing products may be the goal of an acquisition. Purchase of a competitor serving other geogrpahic areas may serve this marketing objective. Effective planning is important in geographical expansion, since personnel retention will probably be a necessity for success.

Effective employee relations are necessary to ensure a successful geographic expansion. Successful remote operations require excellent personnel, effective organizations, and appropriate management control. Management information systems and management performance goals should be closely reviewed to establish effective transition plans.

In-depth discussion with the "new venture" management team by the acquiring company senior executive will minimize acquisition disruption. Personnel risk is higher in a geographic expansion, since we are dealing with a remote facility. This can be seen in Exhibit 9.3.

Acquisition of an entire company may result in serious disruption in daily activity in both companies if not completed properly. The buyer must understand that there may initially be serious mistrust and apprehension. This can be controlled through careful planning and appointment of a task force leader who consistently encourages positive relationships. This will be discussed later in the chapter.

Vertical Integration

Vertical integration involves product line expansion either progressing closer to the "raw material" state or to the final "end product" stage. Many examples of vertical integration have occurred during the past few years, and could include a steel company purchasing iron ore mines. In this instance, the acquiring company was integrating toward the raw material source. "End product" integration occurred, for example, when Texas Instruments expanded its product line into the consumer electronics area.

Vertical integration involves substantially more risk than product line or geographic expansion, since the venture is in a different business environment. The acquired business must be thoroughly evaluated, considering primary risk areas such as customer service (manufacture and distribution) and personnel. Both risks are high in this expansion, since manage-

Exhibit 9.1
Product Line Analysis

(000's)

	QUARTERS							
	1	2	3	4	5	6	7	8
Sales - Gross	100	100	300	700	1000	1000	1200	
Less: Substitution			50	100	250	300	300	
Net Sales	100	100	250	600	750	700	900	
Gross Profit								
Gross	50	50	150	350	500	500	600	
Substitution Effect			15	30	75	90	90	
Total	50	50	135	320	425	410	510	

Expenses							
Sales - Direct		20	50	75	200	200	250
Distribution costs							
Whse	20	20	20	30	30	30	40
Delivery	5	5	10	20	25	25	30
Packaging	5	5	15	20	25	25	25
Advertising	20	20	30	100	75	50	50
Administrative		20	20	20	20	20	30
Subtotal	50	70	125	265	375	350	425
Expense Saving				10	30	30	30
Net Expense	50	70	125	255	345	320	395
Contribution Margin	0	-20	10	65	80	90	115

Exhibit 9.2
Risk Analysis

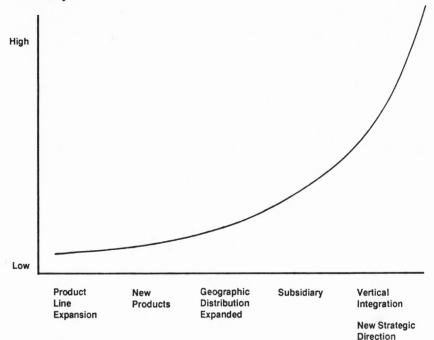

Exhibit 9.3
Risk Analysis: Personnel

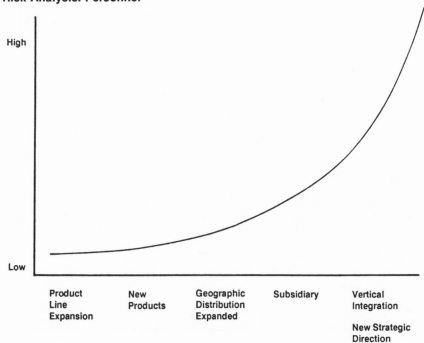

ment is less famliar with the environment. Exhibit 9.2 indicates higher combined personnel/customer service risk than other expansions discussed. All segments of the operation must be thoroughly reviewed to ensure that a complete plan is developed.

If the vertical integration is a purchase of a complete business operation, careful review of existing personnel, policies, and procedures is essential to ensure that the plan considers and resolves appropriate risks. Although this type of venture represents a high risk venture, the risks are less than that of a strategic direction change.

New Strategic Direction

Exhibit 9.4 illustrates a total risk analysis.

A new strategic direction may involve the most risk of all possible acquisitions evaluated. In such an acquisition, the company has not been actively involved in the business purchased. This expansion entails customer service risks (manufacturing and distribution) and personnel risk, but to a much higher degree than vertical integration.

Exhibit 9.4
Total Risk Analysis

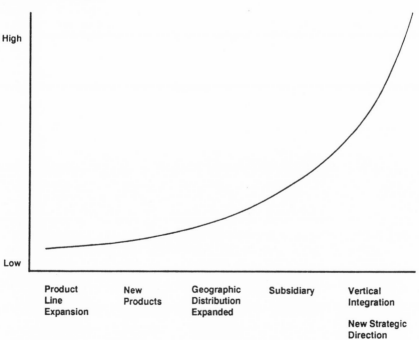

Personnel evaluations and organization structure are critical to the successful integration of these operations. Such a strategic venture may be successful only if the acquired company management continues in place. The transition plan may require a remote "hands-off" procedure.

A new "strategic direction" purchase will require a tolerant acquiring company management, which will accommodate the unfamiliar and trust the acquired company management.

INTEGRATION PLANS

We will not thoroughly review the purchase price evaluation of a new acquisition, except to establish that the "out-of-pocket" costs paid to the seller are not the only cost of acquisition. The acquisition may require either very little or extremely intense efforts by the acquiring company's management. This, while it may not be easily quantified, may represent a major portion of cost.

This investment represents a venture opportunity cost, since management efforts are diverted from other areas. This should be estimated in the initial planning before acquisition.

Integration planning is one of the most important features of an acquisition. Companies may establish a "buyer's team," which has responsibility to finalize a purchase and immediately pass operations control directly to management. However, development of an implementation team, and a well-prepared transition plan will help ensure that effective integration will occur. An integration team must be established to ensure that communications are clear and directed to the appropriate individuals. A complete plan and periodic reporting by the project team will help to avoid any possible culture shock.

Effective planning includes defining a transition team, evaluating personnel, and formulating a task-oriented plan and checklist.

Definition of a Transition Team

Team composition will depend on the type of transaction. The transition team leader must be a senior level executive who is committed to delivering a successful acquisition. A successful acquisition is one which is "purchased within plan," resulting in an established, fully integrated operation. A senior level executive will reinforce the fact that the acquisition is important to the company. The executive should have operating responsibility for the successful integration of the business into the existing environment.

The team should include representatives from marketing, manufacturing, distribution, personnel, and finance. The team must be a highly motivated, results-oriented task force *that will deliver the objective.*

Development of a team matrix will identify functional needs. Although it would be good if the best employees were always assigned to acquisitions, a matrix provides a systematic method of assigning individuals based on risks (see Exhibit 9.5). For example, personnel, legal, and finance are not critical team members in the product line expansion discussed in Exhibit 9.1. Through analysis of the potential acquisition, risks and opportunities can be identified.

Initial impressions of the team requirements may indicate that participants from each major discipline would overwhelm the acquired company. This could easily occur if the team charter is not properly defined. Suggestions for the charter include the following:

1. If the company is well-managed and successful, acknowledge that fact, and allow it to continue to manage basically as it has in the past, provided this meets your strategic objectives.

2. Require the team to integrate the new operation within a realistic, specified time period.

3. Require the team to become thoroughly familiar with the basic operation, and to become an empathetic part of their management team.

4. Provide "corporation" counsel, which can be used as background by the acquired company for complete future integration.

5. Do not interfere with a well-managed company just because you own it! Remember that the team purpose is to support and integrate.

6. Do not ignore the needs of the purchased company. In some situations due to limited capital under previous management, opportunities may have been missed. Be sure that the corporation's resources are considered in all facets of decision making.

7. Do not overlook opportunities to demonstrate the value of the new operations to the company. Each positive contact will renew the enthusiasm and reconfirm the decision to purchase.

Team member personality traits should include all the positive elements of a key executive. Such traits include: desire to succeed, creativity, high energy level, eagerness to function as a team member, expertise in chosen field and willingness to develop additional skills, and ability to function in a high pressure environment.

After definition of the matrix and clear identification of specialties required, the team leader must consider personnel available. Remember, however, that personnel needs must be satisfied, but not necessarily by in-house personnel. If needs are critical and qualified staff are sparse, you should consider outside consultants. Consultants are always available in offshore operations, but the costs may be very high.

Exhibit 9.5
Team Matrix

	Rank in Priority Order		
	1 (High)	2 (Medium)	3 (Low)
Marketing			
Advertising			X
Market Research		X	
Strategic Planning		X	
Prod Line Management	X		
Packaging Design	X		
Manufacturing			
Engineering		X	
Planning	X		
Process Control		X	
Distribution			
Management		X	
Traffic			X
Purchasing Control			X
Personnel			
Pension Planning			X
Benefit Administration		X	
Salary/Compensation	X		
Training			X
Finance			
Accounting			X
Tax	X		
Treasury Adminstration	X		
Insurance Risk Analysis			X
Legal			
Patent	X		
General Counsel		X	
Product Labeling			X

Personal Evaluations

Personnel risks have been highlighted in several exhibits. These risks exist because a new venture may be in unusual areas (either product lines or geographic regions) when compared to the core business. In all cases, if the acquiring company management is unfamiliar with the environment, it is essential that management talent at the acquired company be retained.

A formal evaluation of each target company key executive should be prepared within a specified time (e.g., six months) to ensure that the pool of acquired talents is properly assessed. This will be helpful not only to reflect interest in the new venture, but also to further emphasize that quality management will receive rewards. As the evaluation is completed, all executives should be ranked based on talents and personal traits. While some of the executives will be instrumental in maintaining the new venture operations over the long term, others may represent talent that may be useful in other areas of the core business. This presents an opportunity to cross-train or develop new techniques in the core organization.

Personnel evaluations assume that a new venture is a successful operation. If the new venture is expected to be a turnaround venture, evaluations are also essential, but the purpose is to ensure that the correct team for turnaround is in place.

Task-Oriented Plan

Preparation of a well-developed plan defining specific objectives for a venture is important. The team must understand the results expected, and the rewards should be established accordingly. Returns from the venture may not necessarily be consistent (e.g., return on sales of 25 percent) with that of the core business, since future growth may be the reason for the purchase. A well-publicized plan, with full disclosure of primary objectives, will ensure that if goals have been met, success will prevail. The plan must be developed and endorsed by the project team.

Plan deliverables should include objectives other than financial milestones. A well-prepared plan would identify essential business elements necessary for complete integration and could include a brief Gannt chart separating key areas of management influence (see Exhibit 9.6).

This type of planning allows for highly descriptive and easily reported progress. Note that financial targets have not been included. Many plans may concentrate only on "the numbers." While dollar returns are important considerations, these returns should not be the only focus of the operation.

For example, if a new venture required final development of an electrical device, so that UL (Underwriter's Laboratory) approval could be obtained before introduction, the plan should have targets other than sales (see Exhibit 9.7). Rather than review monthly financial results, a more

Exhibit 9.6
Acquisition Plan

```
                                      W E E K S

                                  1     2     3     4     5     6     7     8

MARKETING
----------

Review complete product line   XXXXXXXXXXXXXXXXXXXX

Assess cannibalization               XXXXXXXXXXXXXXXXXX

Define integration plan                    XXXXXXXXXXXXXXXXXXXXX

Review with marketing management                       XXXX

Develop advertising theme                                    XXXXXXXXX

Develop advertising copy                                        XXX XXXXXXXXX

Identify advertising media                                   XXX

Review with management                                       XXXXXXXXX
```

Exhibit 9.7
Example: Device Approval

```
                                      W   E   E   K   S
                                  -------------------------------------
                                    1   2   3   4   5   6   7   8   9
                                  -------------------------------------

Design specifications required    XXX XXXXXXXXX

Obtain approval of design             XXXXXXXXX

Develop cost estimates                XXXXXXXXX

Begin prototype development               XXXXXXXXXXXXXXXXXXXXX

Assess prototype                                  XXXXXXXXX

Modify designs; discuss with marketing                XXX XXXXXXXXX

Begin testing                                             XXXXXXXXXXXXXXXXXXXXX

Evaluate testing                                              XXXXXXXXXXXXXXXXXXXXX

Establish production standards                                    XXXXXXXXXXXXXXXXXXXXXXXX
```

123

appropriate review would include progress toward the prime goal—development and acceptance of the product.

DEVELOPMENT THROUGH DISTRIBUTORS

Improved product lines and geographic expansions can be completed without ownership. In each case, licenses or contractual obligations can be established to ensure that the company objectives (product line integration, expanded market share) can be achieved. As with the purchase of these items discussed earlier, a task force should be established to ensure that all considerations have been reflected in the final negotiated contract.

As with any acquisition, it should be understood that the business deal will benefit both parties. Parameters should be established before any negotiations begin. Minimum business criteria should be established and investigated before any formal negotiations occur. Examples of criteria which should be considered are similar to "acquisition" criteria, and should include: market share, product line analysis (competitive, expanded vertical integration, new strategic direction), customer goodwill, and sales force or distribution organization. As these criteria are reviewed, it is important that each item is evaluated to determine potential impact on the negotiation.

In addition, a team leader should be appointed to ensure that all the features negotiated in the contracts have been properly considered in ongoing operations. Checklists of obligations of both the vendor/distributor and the base company should be developed to ensure that all the negotiations result in fully implemented features. These checklists should be monitored periodically.

SUMMARY

New ventures can be highly profitable for a business if properly planned. It is not enough to establish a "buy team," pay cash, and assume a new venture will be successful. More important planning issues must be considered for a venture to be successful. We have discussed several types of new ventures and inherent risks associated with each.

Effective planning and management analysis will minimize the risks and improve the chances for successful ventures. Proper planning will also help quantify management time invested and provide a better basis for opportunity evaluation.

Personnel risks have been highlighted as a major concern in all areas other than product line expansion. Management must attend to these risks as well as profit and loss issues during any transition period.

Expansion through distributor operations must be carefully considered, since these distributors represent the company. If business character or operating methods are not consistent with the company, discord may result. Distributor agreements must be thoroughly evaluated to ensure that proper business expansion occurs.

CHAPTER 10

BASELINE FORECASTING: A SIMPLE APPROACH TO PLANNING

Forecasting in the international environment can be confusing and cumbersome. Currency translation rates, multiple locations and product lines, and periodic revisions may require so many "forecast amounts" that the objective of the forecast may be lost in volumes of data.

The objective must be to develop an estimate of the results and to define specific action plans to achieve the results.

During the past few years corporations have focused on budgeting techniques known as "zero base budgeting." This technique is probably the most complete review of an operation. However, it requires close coordination and extensive commitment from all personnel.

Management may not have available resources to properly complete a "zero base budget." An alternative to zero base budgeting is a technique called "baseline forecasting." This can best be completed by middle management using broad trends in each phase of the business operation. Areas which require review include: sales/cost of sales (definition of products, product families, distribution channels, regions or sales territories) and expense reviews (fixed expense definition, variable expense definition).

Note that only key components of the business mix have been highlighted. As we proceed with a baseline forecast, specific factors within these broad categories that initially appear insignificant may develop in importance. Management must always concentrate on the overall objective and not become bogged down with insignificant detail.

This baseline forecasting technique has been used effectively in individual subsidiary operations ranging from $2 million to $25 million of annual sales, with from 500 to 5000 customers. It can be used for a mix of countries, concentrating only on values or operations that are significant or on specific expenses within larger operations. General guidelines to the technique and examples follow. The objective of baseline forecasting is to improve tactical or short-term operating results through identification of targeted, results-oriented spending plans.

This chapter will identify personnel and organization required to implement a baseline forecast; review methods to establish a baseline for sales and expenses, and discuss preparation of results-oriented reports to describe progress toward forecast objectives.

DEFINITION OF PERSONNEL

Personnel in all organizations are essential for the proper execution of a baseline forecasting procedure. However, we should understand that the forecasting technique may be considered unusual, simply because it is a change. In order to properly implement the system it is essential that an effective team is defined. There are several considerations in selecting an effective installation team:

1 . The proper organizaton level must participate.
2. The technique requires a "champion"—an innovative individual who can overcome obstacles and deliver the results.
3. The correct departments must participate to establish accountability.

Organization Levels

A new forecasting technique must be endorsed by senior level executives in any organization. A new system can be implemented only through selection of the installation team from a relatively high organizational level. For example, it would be difficult to implement the system using a financial analyst as the project director. Proper assignment will provide the necessary organizational endorsement and also provide the essential staff to perform the analytical tasks.

The Champion

A "champion" is an individual who will not accept defeat in completing a major task. The champion enlists the necessary formal and informal resources to ensure success. Such a champion will generally be hard driving yet politically astute. Such an individual must be involved in the basic development process, and also in each phase of the project completion.

The champion will select the appropriate team and instill a feeling of success in each phase of the project. This is accomplished through proper goal setting, intermediate measurement points, and periodic staff meetings. If a champion is selected and allowed to function with reasonable autonomy, the project will most likely be successful.

Departments

A brief examination of the purpose of baseline forecasting will result in the conclusion that organization performance will improve with minimal incremental effort. However, it should be clear that this is not just a financial exercise. Several key departments must be included in the exercise. These may include:

Marketing. Sales analysis and development of marketing plans to achieve certain targets should be developed and endorsed by the marketing function. Coordination and assignment of sales and marketing resources will be completed during the baseline forecast.

Finance. Financial control of the forecasting process can most effectively be achieved with the finance department as the central control over the forecasting process. The department also has the capacity to analyze "what if" alternatives and assist other departments in developing plans.

Manufacturing. Manufacturing schedule changes may be required, based on the forecasts developed. Additional resources may be required or redirected to higher priority projects. Close coordination with sales and marketing will ensure that required products will be produced.

Sales Operations. Sales efforts may be realigned to different priorities in the short term. New product introductions or emphasis on specific existing products or territories may require in-depth planning. Sales participation will ensure commitment to delivering the final objectives.

Each organization is different. Departments involved in the forecasting process are those required to implement incremental plans. A careful review of the organization should be completed at each forecast to ensure that appropriate departments have been included. It is critical that the personnel involved should have sufficient authority to commit resources and work through alternative or contingency plans.

BUSINESS REVIEW

Once the forecast team has been established, analysis can begin. The foundation of baseline forecasting is a thorough understanding of the underlying business trends. These can be either sales or spending trends. The business must be reviewed based on discrete business features and should be segmented into manageable "analysis areas."

Sales Analysis

Baseline forecasting can best be completed in sales and marketing operations. Manufacturing department forecasts can also be completed using the baseline method, but may not result in improved forecast control due to the limited variable or discretionary spending flexibility.

Proper sales analysis will define a baseline sales level that can serve as a foundation for incremental spending plans. Analysis will concentrate on period sales (sales per month or per week), and can be segmented in any way appropriate for the operation. Examples of sales segments follow:

Geographic	Product Line	Distribution Channel
District	Type	Wholesale
Country	Group	Retail
Region	Family	Distributor

Geographic segments should be established for all operations. In international operations, segmentation can include broad classification (such as total Latin America) or smaller segments (such as separate countries—Panama, Colombia, Peru, Ecuador, etc.). Within a country, sales regions (Panama—Free Zone; City of Panama) may also be appropriate. Sales/marketing management must review and define appropriate segments.

Definition of product categories will assist in the development of meaningful plans. Product categories should be defined to ensure that sales/marketing efforts are targeted, not fragmented, to achieve the best results.

Again, careful analysis of the product distribution channel is essential to ensure that marketing plans achieve the maximum benefit.

These forms of general segmentation should be done before baseline forecasting so that targeted spending plans to increase benefit can be developed.

Regional Sales

Each "segment" (geographic, product line, distribution channel) may be a management responsibility within the organization. For example, in geographic segmentation, a region may include several countries which combined are the responsibility of the regional sales manager. The regional sales manager should be familiar enough with the operation to establish a norm or baseline for each manageable segment. This can be accomplished through review of monthly or periodic values reported for the segment. The review can be either financial summaries or perhaps a graphic presentation (see Exhibit 10.1).

Exhibit 10.1
Regional Sales Summary

SALES - EUROPE   (000's $)

COUNTRY	JAN	FEB	MAR	APR	MAY	JUN	JUL	AUG	SEP	Targ
Austria	12	11	11	11	14	12	12	10	9	11
England	60	70	60	66	68	75	68	67	70	66
Germany	55	45	44	47	55	57	60	55	66	58
Italy	78	79	77	80	86	89	85	86	90	86
Spain	55	45	46	51	51	46	50	50	48	50
Total	260	250	238	255	274	279	275	268	283	271

The regional sales summary lists monthly sales results in a simple form. This is done to highlight monthly business trends. The final column, labeled "Targ," is the target performance for the country. The "target" is established through observation of monthly sales to identify the likely level of sales volume. This means that without any incremental stimulus (advertising programs, sales incentives, new product introductions, etc.), we could expect the target sales performance from the respective country. This information could be further refined to identify *weekly trends* within each month.

Exhibit 10.2 is a summary of average weekly sales. The weekly sales trends summary further demonstrates that trends exist in every sales operation. Weekly trends and seasonal patterns can be more easily identified through these simplified presentations. Graphs can also be used to identify sales trends by country, region, and so on. Graphs allow for immediate recognition of trends. These techniques are not statistically sophisticated, but rather simple approaches to control the sales operation. Exhibit 10.3 represents a simple graph for Germany.

Note that while there is variability in the weekly sales rates, a sales level of "12" is a good estimate of a baseline. The baseline is the minimum expected sales level, without incremental effort. This graphic analysis could also be extensively analyzed using regression analysis techniques,

Exhibit 10.2
Weekly Sales Trends

```
SALES - EUROPE   (000's $)
```

COUNTRY	JAN	FEB	MAR	APR	MAY	JUN	JUL	AUG	SEP	Targ
Austria	3	3	2	3	3	2	3	3	2	3
England	15	17	12	16	17	15	17	17	14	15
Germany	14	11	9	12	14	12	15	14	13	12
Italy	20	20	15	20	22	18	21	21	16	19
Spain	14	11	9	13	13	9	12	13	9	11
Total	66	62	47	64	69	56	68	68	54	60

Exhibit 10.3
German Sales

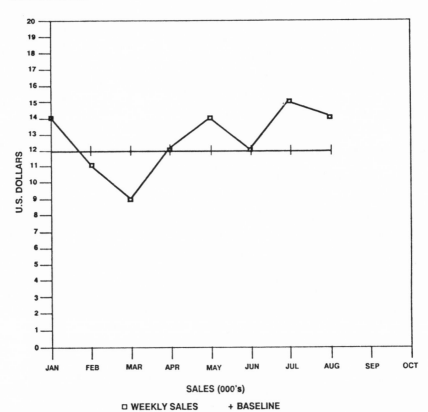

SALES (000's)

□ WEEKLY SALES   + BASELINE

which would also result in a certain predictable sales trend. If regression analysis techniques are available, they should be considered. However, simple math averages should suffice in most sales operations. The graphic analysis could also be extended to any of the segments defined, such as product type, distribution channel, or other geographic segmentation.

Similar analyses should be prepared for any significant sales statistic. It is important that management "step back" from the operation to identify and understand the trends that *must be* evident in all operations. The trends are there; you must identify and interpret them.

Trend identification is the key to developing plans for incremental programs (such as special pricing programs, advertising programs, sales incentive programs, etc.). Incremental programs and their control will be discussed later.

Product Analysis

Most companies cannot prosper with the sale of only a single product. It is important that the products offered be reviewed and classified in proper groups. This can be done with manufactured products, services, and so on. Key product groups should be defined by the marketing department (or similar functional group). Product groups can be sub-divided into key product types.

For example, an electronics manufacturer may have one thousand consumer products for sale. The monthly or quarterly activity of each product should be reviewed with marketing management, production management, and inventory control personnel. It is likely that out of the one thousand items sold, there are no more than 25 key products, which may be in very few product groups. A key product is defined as one with high volume activity, high total profit contribution initially, and high potential profit contribution. During product analysis, it is important to concentrate on the products contributing the most to operations to establish the baseline. This may be completed through product listing or grouping in product families.

Exhibits 10.4 and 10.5 indicate two types of product sales analyses. Note that this list is not necessarily in any specific order. A more meaningful summary of product sales may be by type of equipment, as noted in Exhibit 10.5.

Note that by grouping in similar product lines (Format B), the forecasting in total dollar sales becomes much simpler. In fact, the sales forecast may be limited to two product lines, such as TV equipment and stereo equipment. Baseline sales analysis should *concentrate only on significant items*. Analyses can be completed for territories, countries, customers, and distribution channels.

Identifying meaningful groups of information for managers will help to ensure that a reasonable, appropriate forecast is prepared.

Exhibit 10.4
Product Summary by Type

Format A

P E R I O D

(000's U.S. Dollars)

	1	2	3	4	Total
TV - Mono	-	40	-	-	40
TV - stereo	-	-	12	-	12
TV - portable	-	-	-	12	12
Stereo - cons	-	-	40	-	40
Stereo - port	4	14	-	-	18
Tuners	2	17	-	-	19
Tape Decks	25	14	-	-	39
VCR - stereo	10	18	18	-	46
VCR - mono	-	-	25	-	25
Total	41	103	95	12	251

================================

EXPENSE

Expense analysis can take many forms. Two primary methods will be reviewed in this chapter: (1) trend analysis, and (2) fixed/variable. Each of these methods will be considered in the baseline expense analysis. The objective of baseline expense analysis is to develop incremental spending plans to achieve specific returns for the company.

In order to effectively analyze only the incremental programs, the company should review all expense levels annually, and use this as the basis for limited analysis for the remainder of the year. Similar to the sales analysis, spending patterns are predictable based on history and basic knowledge of future operations. The analysis will concentrate on review of

Exhibit 10.5
Product Summaries—Product Line

Format B

P E R I O D

	1	2	3	4	TOTAL
Stereo					
Console	-	-	40	-	40
Portable	4	14	-	-	18
Tuners	2	17	-	-	19
Tape Deck	25	14	-	-	39
Subtotal	31	45	40	-	116
TV					
Mono	-	40	-	-	40
Stereo	-	-	12	-	12
Portable	-	-	-	12	12
VCR - Mono	-	-	25	-	25
VCR - Ster	10	18	11	-	46
Subtotal	10	58	55	12	135

financial statement classifications, which generally group expenses func-tionally (e.g., selling, administrative, marketing, etc.). Note that these will generally closely align to the functional departments discussed above.

Analysis will be similar to the sales trend analysis. Graphic presenta-tions and perhaps schedules listing monthly values should be used to identify these trends. Again, statistical techniques such as regression analysis could be used and would be more statistically valid. However, these methods may not be available. Simple analysis will be adequate for baseline forecasting.

Cost/expenses must be reviewed to determine a baseline cost/expense amount. These are "fixed" or committed expenses for the operating organization. Baseline expenses should be segregated by the fixed/variable classification based on type of service activity.

Fixed expenses can be defined as those expenses that:

—Have an existing commitment such as leases or insurance contracts
—Are in the current base of operations (existing administrative or sales force)
—Are required to support basic, previously defined fixed expenses (fringe benefits for existing force, utilities, basic phone/telex charges)

Variable expenses could be defined as:

—Discretionary spending that can be shifted to other areas based on management decision
—Additions to fixed expense to support the incremental benefits defined in the forecasting plans

Baseline expense forecasting will concentrate on service activities grouped by function. Note that we will again try to group individual items into management action items. Several types of service categories would include:

Selling	Administrative	Advertising
Direct selling	Bookkeeping/accounting	Consumer advertising
Distributor costs	Credit and collection	Advertising development costs
Phone/mail sales	General administration	Media costs
Order entry	Occupancy	

Distribution
  Packaging
  Freight out		

Training and seminars		
Market research		

Financial management should complete an expense review identifying fixed and variable expenses for each service category or service department. This will have a dual purpose:

1. The review will establish a fixed expense base for future forecast and operating plans.

2. The review will identify discretionary or incremental expenses that may contribute to the success of these baseline plans.

Review of monthly or weekly expense trends should result in the "target" baseline level of spending. Depending on the time available, this target can be established at the country level, the functional level, or perhaps the individual service level (e.g., "automobile expense"). Once the baseline is established, development of discretionary or variable spending can be completed.

Exhibit 10.6 reflects selling expenses for several countries. Note that Italy experiences a large increase in expense in March. Review of management reports should indicate that some unusual activity occurred. This may be the result of a product introduction or exceptional sales effort in Italy. Such product introductions or incremental sales efforts are *exactly* what we will plan in the next segment. The summaries can also be completed by country to indicate special expense trends (see Exhibit 10.7).

As we review the above schedules, we should be careful to understand historical trends and also the business reason for any unusual fluctuations. These can be done through brief notes on the summaries or succinct attached narratives. Financial summaries and observation analysis are the keys to a successful baseline forecast.

Again we will review a graphic analysis of the expense summaries. Note the unusual fluctuations and the notes on the graphs. Keeping the analysis simple is the only method for proper analysis. Analysis of Exhibit 10.8 shows "spikes" in spending as previously noted in the expenses—selling

Exhibit 10.6
Expenses—Selling

COUNTRY	JAN	FEB	MAR	APR	MAY	JUN	JUL	AUG	SEP	Targ
Austria	3	3	4	3	3	4	3	4	4	3
England	12	16	16	12	11	13	12	13	17	12
Germany	10	10	11	14	13	11	10	11	13	10
Italy	16	17	22	18	16	24	24	16	17	18
Spain	12	13	13	12	14	14	12	12	14	13
Total	53	59	66	59	57	66	61	56	65	57

Exhibit 10.7
P&L Expenses

DESCRIP	JAN	FEB	MAR	APR	MAY	JUN	JUL	AUG	SEP	Targ
Selling										
Salaries	8	8	10	8	8	10	8	8	10	9
Fringe	2	2	2	2	2	2	2	2	2	2
Travel	1	2	2	1	-	2	2	1	1	1
Displays	2	2	-	1	3	3	3	3	2	3
Samples	1	1	3	2	1	3	3	-	-	1
Commission	2	2	5	4	2	4	4	2	2	2
Other	-	-	-	-	-	-	-	-	-	-
Total	16	17	22	18	16	24	24	16	17	18
Advertising										
Salaries	2	2	2	2	2	2	2	2	2	2
Fringe	-	-	1	-	-	1	-	-	1	1
Travel	-	1	-	-	-	2	2	-	-	-
Development	2	1	-	-	-	1	-	-	-	-
Media										
Print	-	-	3	-	-	2	3	-	-	-
Televis	-	-	-	-	-	-	-	-	-	-
Radio	-	-	-	-	-	-	-	-	-	-
Brochures	-	-	2	-	-	2	1	-	-	-
Total	4	4	5	2	2	8	9	3	3	3

Exhibit 10.8
Expense Control

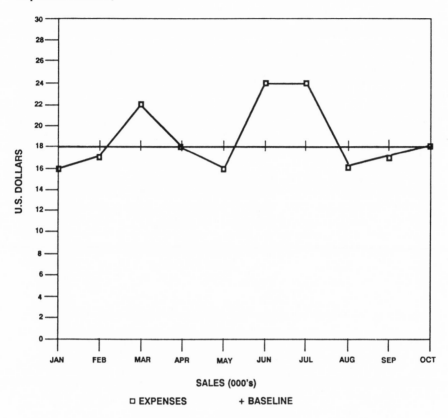

schedule. Simple explanations should be required for this unusual spending, such as "implemented incremental commission plan. . . ."

PREPARATION OF THE FORECAST

Sales Analysis

We have now had the opportunity to review a technique of analysis that is simple—observation of trends. We have also identified a method for identifying a baseline trend which focuses on monthly or weekly trends, and can be used as the baseline for preparation of the forecast. The forecast is *not just a numbers exercise*. We intend to develop action plans to ensure that the financial results can be achieved. The sales baseline identified in the regional sales summary will be used as the basis for the incremental sales forecast.

Exhibit 10.9 presents a "target baseline" for Italy. We will assume that the baseline for a month's sales is 86. A worksheet should help develop the forecast. The worksheet will begin with the baseline and define specific incremental programs to increase sales. These incremental programs will also be covered in expense summaries.

The worksheet in Exhibit 10.10 refers to three incremental plans that should be developed in more detail by responsible managers. However, the format on the worksheet should be closely noted. We have referred to specific plans and specific expected results. As the forecast period expires, the system should provide reporting against these financial objectives. Of course, the plans themselves should have specific activities outlined to ensure performance. Such plans could include:

Due Date	Name	Description
8/10	Smith	Develop compensation plan; review with Jones
8/20	Jones	Final review by Jones
9/6	Jones	Review with personnel and sales
9/12	Jones	Deliver to print shop for typeset
9/22	Jenkins	Final Review before sales meeting
10/1	Jenkins	Present to sales meeting

Specific dates and managers' names have been identified in the plan. This establishes firm accountability for tasks to be completed, not just financial values to be recorded. Progress reporting against the above objectives would include financial statements indicating progress, as well as a written progress report identifying status against the objectives. Reporting frequency should be determined on a case-by-case basis, but generally once-a-month will be appropriate.

Expenses

Spending plans can be developed in similar ways. Once the baseline has been identified, incremental spending plans should be prepared to obtain the expected results. Again, both the description of the task and the expected cost should be defined. Periodic reports—probably monthly—should be prepared. Exhibit 10.11 is an example of an expense summary.

As with sales planning, incremental spending plans should be developed that focus on business activity as well as expense. Such plans should include responsibilities, description of tasks, and dates to perform. Periodic status reports (e.g., monthly) should be required to monitor task performance and spending. Exhibit 10.12 is an example of a combined plan and status report. Simple planning and monitoring through Gannt charts or similar presentations will provide the necessary control to effectively deliver a completed project on time.

Exhibit 10.9
Italian Sales

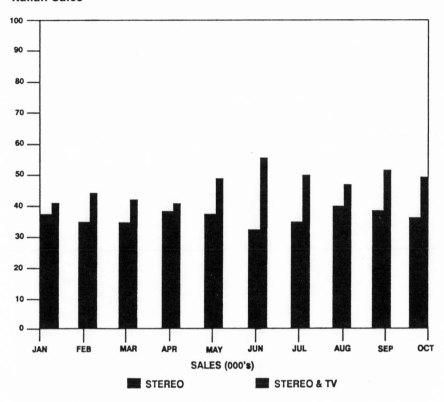

Exhibit 10.10
Baseline Forecast—Sales Plan

Description	April	May	June	Total
Baseline established	86	86	86	258
Introduce new tape player	2	3	9	14
Intro new sales incentive plan	-	2	2	4
Intro advertising program				
- print campaign	-	4	-	4
-radio campaign	-	4	6	10
TOTAL SALES	88	99	103	290

Exhibit 10.11
Baseline Forecast—Expense Plan

(000'S)

Description	April	May	June	Total
Baseline established	18.0	18.0	18.0	54.0
Introduce new tape player	2.0	3.0	9.0	14.0
Intro new sales incentive plan	-	0.5	0.5	1.0
Intro advertising program				
- develop ad campaign	1.5	-	-	1.5
- obtain internal approval	-	-	-	-
- test market ad	0.5			0.5
- run the ad		2.0	2.0	4.0
TOTAL EXPENSES	4.0	5.5	11.5	21.0

SUMMARY

Baseline forecasting is a simple approach to complex business situations. The key to its successful implementation is review at a high level. The manager cannot become consumed with detail. A broad approach may be the only way to avoid being overcome by the international environment. We have defined members of the organization who should be involved in the implementation, and also the necessary "champion" to guide the organization through the baseline technique. These individuals exist in all organizations.

After selection of the implementation team, we have reviewed simple financial summaries. Again, we have focused primarily on the most significant operational issues. We have reviewed significant sales identified by country, region, product, or product family. The secret to success is that we have examined meaningful management data at a reasonable level of detail. The specific data to be examined cannot be defined for the operating manager within this chapter, but a thought process has been defined that requires the manager to step back to gain perspective.

Financial summaries and periodic reporting are critical to the successful implementation of the baseline forecasting system. Responsible managers must also be assigned to the team. These people must be willing to endorse the results of the forecast, and also be willing to deliver on the objectives.

Exhibit 10.12
Baseline Forecast—Expense Plan

DESCRIP.	NAME	APRIL				MAY					JUNE				JULY			
		3	10	17	24	1	7	14	21	28	5	12	19	26	2	9	16	23
Develop																		
Sales																		
Incentive																		
Plan	Johns_____*																	
Review																		
and																		
Approve																		
Plan	Jenkins			*														
Introduce																		
Plan	Philmont							*										
Initial																		
Payments																		
Made														*			*	
Cost														500			500	

CHAPTER 11

BUDGETING AND MANAGEMENT RESPONSIBILITIES IN THE INTERNATIONAL ENVIRONMENT

Bugeting is exceptionally difficult in international operations due primarily to currency fluctuation. Assignment of responsibilities for unexpected rate variances, if not done properly, can result in disruptions in the organization. Management performance can be improved through proper assignment of responsibility.

This chapter outlines the rationale to define responsibility for exchange rates in performance measurement, concentrating on operations and treasury responsibility.

The objective is to match the authority to effect results with the responsibility to perform.

Management in the international environment demands unusual flexibility from corporate management, since political and economic conditions change continuously throughout the world. Multinational companies generally have a "portfolio" of country participants in their operations. Regional wars, devaluations, tax adjustments, and so on force management to adapt business methods to local ambient conditions.

Such conditions make it difficult to assign management responsibilities and performance goals. Quantifying and properly measuring international performance has been a difficult task for years. FASB 52 relates specifically to foreign currency translations, allowing corporate management to apply reasonable judgment in reporting offshore performance. This chapter defines a method of goal setting and internal measurements that can be used by multinational organizations. The basic concept is flexibility in goal measurement and definition.

RESPONSIBILITY THEORY

Multinational management needs to establish performance goals that financial statements include: sales, operating earnings, net earnings, and asset management goals (e.g., return on assets, current ratio, fixed asset investment). However, U.S. companies may not provide flexible goal setting for offshore subsidiaries. For example, the devaluations in Mexico decreased the dollar sales value (and gross profits, operating earnings, and net earnings). The "theory of responsibility" will focus on a planning process that can be used to properly motivate management by isolating variables within its control, and holding the management responsible for its performance.

Effective management will assign responsibility to the personnel with the authority to deal with risks and opportunities. Management cannot leave responsibilities "unassigned" since this lack of definition will result in opportunity costs or perhaps realized losses. Flexible management will review vested authority and responsibility.

Offshore management has an opportunity to react within a market to economic, political, or technological change. Management *expects and demands* this flexibility. For example, if an offshore manager were to review prevailing market conditions and identified a 25 percent reduction in competition's pricing yet still maintained his previous pricing policy (because his management goal was to achieve a status quo pricing policy), would he be satisfying the corporate goal? Probably not! The offshore general manager is paid to respond to conditions within his marketing environment. He must interpret conditions, recommend a plan of action considering the changing conditions, and obtain necessary approvals for implementing the plan.

Corporate self-analysis may be required to determine if responsibility and authority are consistent. Does corporate management expect the general manager to be an expert at marketing and international financial management? Is the offshore general manager expected to understand the complete corporate foreign currency exposure? Or corporate dividend policy? Or corporate transfer pricing policy?

If we assign a U.S. dollar profit and loss responsibility (through net earnings) to the general manager, we have assigned each of those responsibilities to the offshore manager as well. Authority to respond to each of these facets of the operation may not be vested in the offshore management. Perhaps, without full knowledge of the corporate exposure (or dividend policy, or transfer pricing policy), authority should not be assigned to the offshore manager.

Authority and responsibility should be assigned to the "knowledge" position, the position with implied authority to perform. Corporate foreign currency exposures and dividend policy are the treasurer's "knowledge" position. Tax policy, dividend planning, and transfer pricing are the chief financial officer's "knowledge" position.

Broad definition of responsibility areas are appropriate. These definitions may not now be used by your company, but should be considered as you develop and assign management responsibilities. Basic definitions include:

1. *Operating Earnings.* Operating earnings represent a business unit's performance. Allocations from headquarters and noncontrollable items (at the division level)—including interest expense and foreign currency gains or losses—may not be considered within a division's control. Industry analysts monitor division operating earnings to better understand performance in the prevailing business conditions within the business units' industry. Operating earnings are generally limited to division controllable expenses. These include sales, cost of sales, selling, general and administrative expenses, advertising, and other division controllable expenses.

2. *Net earnings.* Net earnings represent the true earnings of the corporation—earnings available for distribution to the stockholders. They represent operating earnings less all financial costs, foreign exchange effects (when applicable), and tax. These additional factors are generally monitored and controllable at the corporate treasurer or chief financial officer level.

Performance for each portion of the profit and loss statement should be the responsibility of an individual in the corporation (division president, treasurer, chief financial officer). Each segment of the P&L should be reviewed to identify the "knowledge person" or best person to be assigned responsiblity for the segment.

CURRENCY FLUCTUATION

Foreign currency fluctuations have received attention since 1975 due to the impact of FASB 8. This opinion required foreign currency effects to be recorded in current year net earnings. However, this FASB 8 impact did not fully describe the economic impact of changing foreign currency values. Amended FASB positions were released in FASB 52, which better represents the economic impact of foreign currency fluctuations. Exhibit 11.1 indicates the effects of foreign currency fluctuation on sales, expenses, and operating/net earnings in accordance with FASB 52 regulations.

Note that a 10-percent rate change will result in either a U.S. dollar sales amount of $500 or $450. This rate impact can be seen at each line of the financial statement. Net earnings vary by 22 percent. Foreign exchange rates can significantly change reported U.S. dollar results. Exhibit 11.2 highlights some major currencies and historical rates. Consider the impact on the P & L depicted in Exhibit 11.1.

Exhibit 11.1
Example: Rate Impact

	Budget Loc Curr	Rate @ 0.5	Rate @ 0.45	Variance
Units	10	10	10	
Sales	1,000.00	500.00	450.00	0.10
Cost of Sales	600.00	300.00	270.00	0.10
Gross Profit	400.00	200.00	180.00	0.10
Operating Eaxpenses	250.00	125.00	112.50	0.10
Interest	25.00	12.50	11.25	0.10
Exchange		0.00	7.50	
Profit Before Tax	125.00	62.50	48.75	0.22
Tax	65.00	32.50	25.30	0.22
Profit After Tax	60.00	30.00	23.45	0.22

PLANNING CONCEPT

All events in the world economy cannot be foreseen or necessarily compensated for. However, all management personnel should have the common business sense and motivation to accommodate reasonable changes in the business environment. Based on this, operations should be held accountable for reasonable currency movement. Assignment of a portion of responsibility for foreign currency movement recognizes that each subsidiary operates in an ever changing environment. Competitive, legal, economic, and political factors will change in most markets. It is essential that management adapt to these changes. The planning concept provides that currency risks be assigned to offshore management and corporate management, based on management authority and responsibility. Exhibit 11.3 lists accounts in an income statement and proposes responsibility assignments, based on the "knowledge position."

The corporate treasurer is responsible for financing corporate operations. As a result, he has control and responsibility for company debt (whether in U.S. dollars or foreign currency), foreign currency exposures, and the ratio of short-term and long-term debt. The planning concept provides currency risk to be assigned to the corporate treasurer. Worldwide taxes and tax exposures can be controlled through various corporate financial decisions made by the chief financial officer. These decisions

Exhibit 11.2
History of Translation Rates

Dollars per unit of local currency

	July, 1986	July, 1984	July, 1983	July, 1982
Britain	1.492500	1.327000	1.524700	1.746500
Canada	0.720200	0.753000	0.810700	0.793900
France	0.145000	0.114700	0.128700	0.147800
Ireland	1.395000	1.073700	1.226500	1.412700
Japan	0.006396	0.004116	0.004176	0.003970
Germany	0.468300	0.351600	0.386900	0.411500

include transfer price policy, dividend policy, and offshore legal structures (branch versus subsidiary operation) and so on. The planning
concept provides for a portion of this foreign currency risk to be assigned
to the chief financial officer.

All assignable foreign currency P&L risks have been consciously
assigned to areas within the respective scope of authority:

Offshore Manager: Operating earnings, within negotiated foreign currency
translation rates

Treasurer: Financial costs relating to foreign currency exposure and interest costs

Chief Financial Officer: Tax exposures related to dividend policy, tax rates, and
offshore corporate structures.

Exhibit 11.3
Responsibility Assignments

DESCRIPTION	RESPONSIBILITY
Sales	Operations
Cost of Sales	
at Standard	Operations
Other costs	Operations
Distribution costs	Operations
Gross Profit	Operations
Selling Expenses	Operations
Marketing Expense	Operations
Advertising Expense	Operations
Administrative Expense	Operations
Other Operating Expenses	Operations
Total Operating Expenses	Operations
Interest Expense	Treasury
Exchange Losses	Treasury
Profit Before Tax	
Tax	C.F.O..
Profit After Tax	

It should be noted that although all P&L responsibility has been assigned to responsible parties, P&L risk is not necessarily avoided. Responsibility assignment will provide a better mechanism to manage risks and
quantify expected results under certain conditions. The planning process
requires that all P&L risks/opportunities be assigned to a responsible
individual.

BUDGET PROCESS

In order to effectively monitor and control the listed responsibilities, it
is necessary to prepare short-range and long-range plans (annual budgets,
strategic plans). The corporate treasurer will most likely have the best
available information to project currency movements. Therefore, the corporate treasurer should be responsible for forecasting direction of
exchange rates and perhaps indications of the magnitude of the change.
Rate forecasts are extremely difficult to make, and will have perhaps a
50-percent chance of occurring.

The forecast of translation rates provided by the treasurer should be
reviewed, and finally, after any necessary negotiations, accepted by offshore management. During the discussion, local management must provide insight into economic conditions to obtain additional assurance
about the credibility of the forecasted rates. Local managers should
review forecasted rates in relation to their planned sales and spending
level. Translation rate targets should be established for use in the budgeting process. The rate setting process should result in a certain degree of
comfort about the rates to be used. This will mean that the general
manager and the treasurer are confident that rates will perform within a
certain range. The negotiated rates will result in a commitment by the
offshore general manager to manage the operation to *dollar targets for all
rate variances within the range negotiated.*

Exhibit 11.4 illustrates the planning concept. Note that the "translation
rate" band of operations commitment is both + and − surrounding the
budget target rate. The budget process requires the offshore manager to
commit to delivering a dollar performance for any variance within the
band. These rate sensitivity alternatives should be developed in the planning phase, rather than representing responses to conditions without
thorough review.

For example, an offshore manager may deliver $100 as net earnings if
rates vary from .45 to .55. If actual translation rates vary by + 20 percent, the manager will deliver $110 as net earnings. This agreement
implies that local management can, at its discretion, reinvest $10 of net
earnings in the operation. Exhibit 11.4 highlights the "incremental profit"
opportunity and nonoperations risk. Returns improve dramatically for an
upward revaluing currency. Translation rate negotiations allow the

Exhibit 11.4
Translation Rate Range

Company Risk/Opportunity Analysis
Planning Concept

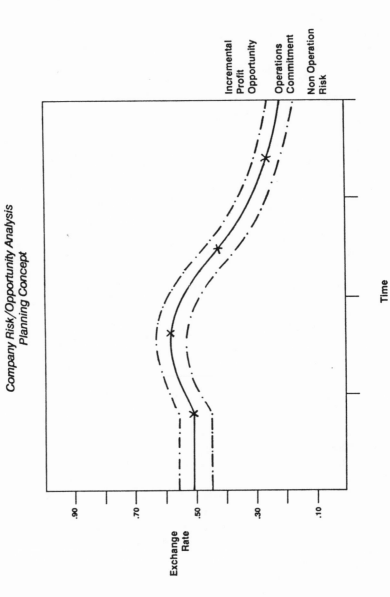

manager to invest a higher proportion of his pretax earnings in the local market. Of course, if the translation rate exceeds the negotiated high point, the manager is expected to return improved profits to the corporation. This also establishes "potential reserves" for the treasurer to use to offset unfavorable variances for transaction losses within his responsibility.

The negotiated rates also provide a lower level cutoff of responsibility for the offshore manager. It should be understood that if the currency falls below those estimated levels, the offshore manager will not be held accountable for resulting variances.

MEASUREMENT PROCEDURES

After an effective management process has been defined, it is essential to establish a reporting system to support measurement. A variance analysis is presented in Exhibit 11.5, which identifies variances by responsibility. Exhibit 11.5 reflects actual local currency and U.S. dollar performance and the budget target rate. The total rate variance includes both operating management responsibility and treasurer, chief financial officer (CFO) responsibility.

Operations responsibility includes a portion of sales and gross profit and operating expenses. Each portion of the P&L statement is analyzed in a traditional manner, in local currency, and translated at the appropriate rate. All translation rate variances are identified (whether operating, treasury, or CFO responsibility). Once isolated, the responsible individual understands the translation rate impact within his scope of control.

Treasury responsibility is limited to financial cost variances (interest expense, exchange). It should be noted that remeasurement gains and losses (under FASB 52) should be considered the treasurer's responsibility. However, since the currency effects are recorded in equity, they are not within the scope of this discussion.

The chief financial officer is responsible for tax rate variances as they relate to combinations of taxable entities, transfer pricing, and dividend policies. Strategies should be defined early in the budget process.

Exhibit 11.5 also includes three sections called noncontrollable. These variances relate to rate variances that cannot be managed by the people identified. The noncontrollable sales variance results from local management's lack of complete flexibility in the local marketplace to accommodate extreme currency fluctuation. For example, a 10-percent currency rate reduction could partially be offset by a 5-percent price increase. The additional 5 percent remains noncontrollable. Other noncontrollable amounts result from the inability to adjust spending or manufacturing costs to the extreme required.

In a well-developed planning process, noncontrollable contingencies should be considered. The variance analysis may identify these factors,

Exhibit 11.5
Variance Analysis

COMPANY "X"
FINANCIAL STATEMENTS

	BUDGET LOCAL CURRENCY	ACTUAL LOCAL CURRENCY	ACTUAL TRANSLATION RATE @ .6	ACTUAL @ BUDGET RATE .5	RATE VARIANCE
UNITS	10	10	10	10	
	---	---	---	---	
SALES	1,000	1,200	720.0	600.0	120.0
COST OF SALES	600	600	360.0	300.0	60.0
	---	---	---	---	---
GROSS PROFIT	400	600	360.0	300.0	60.0
OPERATING EXPENSES	250	260	156.0	130.0	26.0
	---	---	---	---	---
OPERATING EARNINGS	150	340	204.0	170.0	34.0
INTEREST	25	25	15.0	12.5	2.5
EXCHANGE	-	(15)	(9.0)	(7.5)	(1.5)
	---	---	---	---	---
PROFIT BEFORE TAX	125	330	198.0	165.0	33.0
TAX	65	210	126.0		
	---	---	---	---	---
PROFIT AFTER TAX	60	120	72.0	60.0	12.0
	=====	=====	=====	=====	=====

154

SALES VARIANCE:

	L/C	US$

OPERATIONS

Volume: Budget 10 units, Actual 10 units   -0-   -0-

Selling Price:
  Budget 1000 L/C - 10 units = 100 L/C/unit
  Actual 1200 L/C - 10 units = 120 L/C/unit
  Favorable price variance   20
  Total units   10
                                          200   200   100

Operations rate variance: Negotiated maximum rate
(.55) less Budget target rate (.5) times total L/C Sales

  Operations Variance   60
                                                             160

Non Controllable:
Actual rate (.60) less negotiated maximum (.55)
Times total L/C
                                                              60

  TOTAL SALES VARIANCE   220   (A)

(A) = Total sales translation rate variance computed as follows:

	L/C	Rate	US$
Sales-Budget	1,000	.5	500
Sales-Actual	1,200	.6	720
			220

155

Exhibit 11.5 (continued)

COMPANY "X"
NET EARNINGS

	L/C AMOUNT	US$
Operating Earnings Variance:		
Gross Profit Variance:		
Volume = See above		
Selling Price = See above	-0-	
Cost = Budget 600L/C - 10 = 60L/C per unit	200	
Actual 600L/C - 10 = 60L/C per unit		
Variance -0-	-0-	
TOTAL GROSS PROFIT VARIANCE	200 (A)	100.0
Operating Expense Variance:		
Budget 250		
Actual 260		
Unfavorable 10	(10) (B)	(5.0)
variance		
Operating earnings variance [(A) + (B)]	190	95.0
Operations Rate Variance: Negotiated maximum rate		
.55 less Budget		
Target .50 Times L/C Operating earnings	17.0	

OPERATIONS

Non-controllable rate variance: Actual rate less negotiated
      maximum rate (.600-55) times
      L/C operating earnings   17.0

      TOTAL OPERATING EARINGS VARIANCE   129.0   TREASURY

Financial Cost Variance:

   Interest   (2.5)
   Exchange   9.0

      Financial cost variance   6.5

Tax Variance
   Taxable income variance: Actual profit before tax (330L/C)
   Less budget Profit Before Tax (125L/C) times Budget tax
   rate (1-60/125)
   Times Budget exchange rate (.50)   (53.3)   OPERATIONS

Tax rate variance: Actual tax rate less Budget tax rate times
   actual profit before tax times Budget exchange rate   (19.2)   C.F.O.

Non-controllable translation rate variance (actual rate less
   budget rate) times tax amount   (21.0)   TREASURY
                                                             (93.5)

      TOTAL NET EARNINGS VARIANCE   42.0

157

but they may not necessarily be controllable or assignable to individuals or departments.

SUMMARY

While these analyses may initially appear to be cumbersome, management must understand that currency variance cannot be ignored. Translation rate variances, as with any changes in the business environment, must be considered in the management process. Management must not believe that all such risks can be thoroughly managed, but it must understand that the risks cannot and should not be assumed away. This chapter defines an alternative to U.S. dollar budgeting at constant rates. Foreign operation performance can be severely affected by translation rate adjustments. Flexible rate budgeting can provide more effective control over international subsidiaries by planning rate alternatives and identifying responsibility. Through preliminary analysis, management can define the noncontrollable impact and manage its business accordingly.

CHAPTER 12

CONTINGENCY PLANNING IN THE INTERNATIONAL ENVIRONMENT

In the previous chapters, we have discussed planning in organizations, assignment of responsibilities, definition of procedures, and reporting against plans. However, performance rarely matches plan exactly. The world is a dynamic environment. Competent managers *always* have contingency plans prepared to deliver the results. In international operations, contingency plans are essential to survival.

A rationale to develop contingency plans, including discussions of personnel planning, cost control, marketing, and distribution strategies, will be outlined in this chapter. Practical examples of their implementation will also be presented. Contingency plans responding to foreign currency fluctuations will also be discussed. The objective of this chapter is to provide a logical basis for identifying, developing, and implementing contingency plans to deliver results.

The most critical aspect of developing contingency plans is to analyze thoroughly the business risks and identify the most probable points of failure. These risks can take many forms including people, products, customers, and perhaps the legal environment. A formal review program and a "brainstorming session" including all managers in each offshore location should be completed to assure that all high-risk areas of the plan have been identified. These high-risk areas and the contingency plans should be reviewed by area and headquarters management, to assure that all significant high-risk areas have been identified, and to assure that reasonable contingency plans have been developed. It is important that regional and headquarters personnel be consulted in the development of the plans, since certain resources may be available to other management levels to resolve the risk areas identified satisfactorily.

PERSONNEL PLANNING

As noted in the previous chapters, personnel represent a significant investment in the international organization. Unfortunately, due to the extreme distances involved and the social/educational and business background differences,

---

offshore personnel may represent the most significant risks to be evaluated and considered.

Offshore personnel may also represent considerably more investment than U.S. personnel.

As a first step in developing a personnel contingency plan, it is essential to formally review all offshore personnel to identify key players. Specific key responsibilities must be thoroughly understood to ensure that the operation can continue to function, with the implementation of a contingency plan.

Succession Planning

After key personnel and functions have been identified, succession plans should be developed to ensure continuous professional staffing in each operation. Succession plans can take many forms. After a thorough review of the organizations and individuals, management should identify successors within the organization. This review should consider the existing talents and capabilities of people in the organization, as well as the potential talents of personnel. Remember, talented people can be trained if they remain with the company. If these people leave, the company loses. If this review discloses that there are no adequate successors within a specific organization, a review of the broader international or U.S. operations should be performed to identify key players that have abilities suitable to offshore operations.

It is important to understand that many people in the organization are mobile. As you review the entire organization, you should be sure that you consider moving individuals around the world if appropriate.

The last step in succession planning for offshore operations is to consider consultants or bankers as resources to identify backups.

The local offshore organization and the headquarters operation should be considered the primary resource for required backups.

In Exhibit 12.1 the solid line represents permanent replacements throughout the organization. This exhibit presents career growth through an international organization from local management, through regional management, to the world headquarters. This is a healthy environment for all employees.

Stopgap Measures

Personnel contingency plans may not necessarily represent permanent replacement. If temporary problems occur due to illness or termination, temporary backups have an added advantage. If personnel are not accustomed to variety in their present positions, these backups may enjoy a temporary assignment. If permanent replacements are not identified in the personnel review, management should consider identifying temporary replacements.

In Exhibit 12.1, the broken line is directed down through the organization. This represents "stopgap" measures for temporary replacement of individuals in each layer of the organization. Recall that if promotion from within is the norm for the international organization, these individuals should be well versed in the duties and responsibilities for each earlier or more focused operation.

PROFIT & LOSS—CONTINGENCIES

A major concern for all businessmen is the successful achievement of a profit plan. In particular, sales shortfalls, delayed product introduction, changes in distribution channel, effective cost control, and significant devaluation of foreign currency should be the focus of P&L activity.

Cost Control

In chapter 10 we discussed management actions that may occur in a programmed way that can result in achievement of certain planned sales and earnings objectives. These plans can be limited to specific high probability plans, but should also consider secondary business objectives. Remember, if you have established a firm commitment to delivering the plan, you must analyze the components of potential failure—that is, identify the riskiest portion of the sales plans—to develop alternatives for achieving the targets.

Exhibit 12.2 illustrates a "cost gating" concept which should be used in all forecasting and budgeting. Note that as time progresses from month 1 through 10, certain costs are designated as "required activity" (note the solid line). Recall that all marketing expenses generally occur in advance

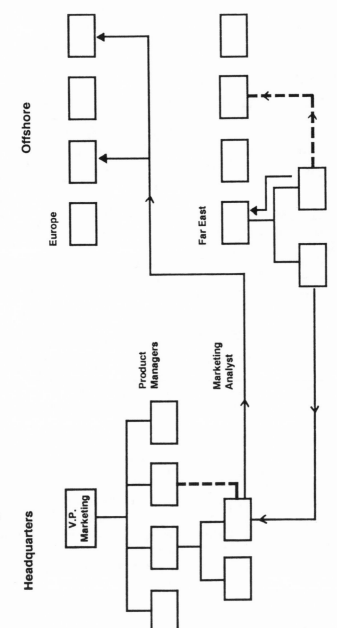

Exhibit 12.1
Succession Planning

Headquarters

Offshore

Europe

Far East

Product Managers

Marketing Analyst

V.P. Marketing

= Potential Move / Temporary Replacements

= Planned Permanent Succession

162

Exhibit 12.2
Cost Gating

	Amount	1	2	3	4	5	6	7
Sales								
Promotion 1	100							
Promotion 2	250							
Promotion 3	50							
Marketing Activity								
Promotion 1	25							
Promotion 2	100							
Promotion 3	30							

of sales activity. The solid line represents sales promotion 1 and extends from month 1 through 3. The potential activity extends through months 4 and 5. The sales line for promotion 1 begins with potential activity in period 2 (note the broken line), while the required activity begins in month 3. This indicates that the trial period that begins in month 2 is the target for revenue increases. If expected sales are not achieved by month 3, spending should be reexamined to determine if the plan is meeting its objectives.

Cost gating must consider "drop-dead" dates—points at which program spending will be discontinued unless certain results are achieved. Similar decisions must be made in sales promotion 2 and 3 if we assume that future sales promotion can be funded only by successful earlier sales promotions.

Delayed Product Introduction

In all new product marketing plans, potential delays in new product introduction should be considered. These items should be considered in "contingency plans" allowing for deferral of certain expenses, and the definition of a "drop dead" date for major project spending. Specific checkpoints should be identified within the plan that identify target spending and management activity levels to measure planned progress. Exhibit 12.3 presents examples of checkpoints and fallback positions developed in anticipation of delays or unforeseen obstacles.

Secondary plans should be developed based on existing high probability factors. For example, delays in development of a "new" product enhancement may trigger implementation of a contingency plan to promote existing products.

Other Marketing Issues

Dynamic marketing organizations will continue to develop new product distribution channels and promotional techniques. Each time a new event is scheduled, an element of risk exists. This risk can occur in all phases of marketing, including product development, customers, distribution channels, market segments, and price.

An effective planner will review each major aspect of the plan to identify risks. Consider some of the following situations, and how outcomes should be reflected in plans:

Calamity Conditions

Delayed Product Introduction

Research, Development, and Engineering (RD&E) development behind schedule for a new product

RD&E development behind schedule for a product enhancement

Regulatory approval not received on schedule

Manufacturing supply not available

Improper stock shipped

Product reclassified to restricted import status

Product duties increased by 50 percent

Customer Base

New distribution channel implementation delayed

Major customer lost

Customer segmentation strategy failed—unable to consolidate with distributor operations

Product buying groups reducing overall margins

Volume discounts/pricing structure creating legal gray market

Advertising

National campaign delayed due to creative work/test market studies

Major competitor preempts the national ad program

Pricing

Competition developed major price reduction campaign

Unanticipated coupons introduced in the market

Contingency Plans—Foreign Currency Fluctuations

Foreign currency fluctuations are perhaps the most unpredictable of all contingencies. Major currency fluctuations can substantially impact sales, cost of sales, and expenses.

The philosophy that *every major negative has a major offsetting positive* must be considered in the development of contingency plans. Recall that in a local subsidiary we are competing in a local market environment that may be unaffected by foreign currency fluctuations.

Currency fluctuations should be considered in all international marketing plans. Exhibit 12.4 demonstrates the significant impact on U.S. dollar returns for a U.S. corporation.

The example illustrates the devaluation of the U.S. dollar from $.50 to $.30 per unit of local currency. The exhibit assumes that the product is manufactured in the United States and has a consistent dollar transfer price or cost of sale. In the devaluation period from period 1 to 2, we move from a profit before tax of $1,250 to a loss of $1,250.

A basic marketing concept of developing "added value" or perceived value may solve the P&L exposure. Contingency planning, when considering the "added value" concept, becomes important.

Exhibit 12.3
Secondary Plans: Fallback Positions

	1	2	3	4	5	6	7	8
SALES								
Product 1	5	5	20	25	50	50	20	20
Product 2			15	15	25	40	40	25
Product 3					30	30	50	50
Subtotal	5	5	35	40	105	120	110	95
Contingency								
Coupon A				20	20			
Complimentary product						40	45	
Subtotal	0	0	0	20	20	40	45	0
Potential Total	5	5	35	60	125	160	155	95

Costs							
Product 1	5	10	20	20	10		
Product 2	5	5	10	10	10	10	
Product 3			10	10	10	10	10
Subtotal	10	15	40	40	30	20	10
Contingency							
Coupon A		12	12				
Complimentary product					25	25	
Subtotal	0	12	12	0	25	25	0
Potential Total	10	27	52	40	55	45	10

Note: Contingency plans will be implemented if initial
programs are not meeting objectives. Note that the
contingencies may result with overall reduced profit,
but may maintain market share.

Exhibit 12.4
Foreign Currency Fluctuation

(000's)

	PERIOD 1		PERIOD 2		PERIOD 3	
	L.C.	US $	L.C.	US $	L.C.	US $
Translation Rate		0.50		0.30		0.30
Sales	25,000	12,500	25,000	7,500	37,830	11,350
Cost of Sales	10,000	5,000	16,670	5,000	16,670	5,000
Gross Profit	15,000	7,500	8,330	2,500	21,160	6,350
Expenses						
Selling	6,900	3,450	6,900	2,070	15,230	4,570
Advertising	1,600	800	1,600	480	1,600	480
G&A	4,000	2,000	4,000	1,200	4,000	1,200
Total	12,500	6,250	12,500	3,750	20,830	6,250
Profit Before Tax	2,500	1,250	(4,170)	(1,250)	330	100

Introduction of the marketing concept in period 3, with higher value added to the customer (i.e., higher selling expenses) will result in higher sales. In this exaggerated example, we can spend twice as much local currency with reduced U.S. dollar impact on U.S. dollar profits. The major negative—the devaluing U.S. dollar—and the U.S. dollar cost of sales seem to be enough to ruin the profitability of the operation. However, the marketing mentality will develop and implement an additional $2,500 marketing investment, or value added, to protect the profitability of the business.

These concepts must be thoroughly understood, and used effectively, to compensate for major unfavorable occurrences. Examples of contingency plans to be used in the devaluing U.S. dollar scenario are major advertising programs, complimentary locally produced merchandise, improved professional training, increased co-op advertising, and improved customer delivery and service.

Each of these marketing alternatives could expand the sales and profitability of the organization. Marketing, sales, and financial management must develop contingency plans to compensate for these unusual events. These are just some of the contingency plans that could be developed to compensate for a major sustained devaluation of the U.S. dollar.

Devaluing local currency may present serious cost of sales pressures to the local currency environment. In this situation, costs related to U.S. dollar-sourced goods should be minimized whenever possible. Reduced free or complimentary products may result from devaluations.

SUMMARY

This chapter has discussed the major pitfalls that may occur in the international operation. The most significant actions that could be taken in any plan include a thorough assessment of all high risk components of the plans before the pitfall occurs. High risk planning factors should be thoroughly reviewed at the local management level to ensure that all managers have considered the impact on potential performance.

Each major "negative" and the contingency plan should be extensively reviewed throughout the levels of the international organization. This will allow for resource allocation by each successive level of management. At the conclusion of the contingency planning process, all major potential adverse events should be scheduled with contingency plans to compensate for their impact.

Although the objective of the process is to resolve all potential negative business implications, management should also understand that all such adversity may not necessarily be offset by a management plan. But at least the "unknowns" impact will be established.

CHAPTER 13

F.O.C.U.S.: A COST REVIEW PROGRAM FOR INTERNATIONAL OPERATIONS

This chapter challenges each employee's understanding of his responsibility to the most important person in the job—the customer. In many large companies it is difficult to establish a link between the function performed by individual departments and the customers.

We will review a framework for the systematic review of departmental or employee functions and their relationship to the customer and the company product. Although designed to be used in a distribution operation, the F.O.C.U.S. program can be applied to a country, region, or individual department. The program has been successfully implemented in various international operations ranging from $5 million to $25 million in annual sales. The results of the reviews include departmental reorganizations, distribution channel changes, strategic pricing changes, and reallocation of employee resources. Although F.O.C.U.S. may appear to be a systematic cost cutting program, it should be considered a *cost targeting* program, which considers "value added" to the company product.

The program is designed to make each segment of the operation more effective, not necessarily more efficient. Doing the correct task moderately well is better than doing the wrong task very well.

The F.O.C.U.S. review can be completed in a short time. The concise program is expected to be a quick, hard hitting, and easily implemented review.

F.O.C.U.S. is an acronym for a general business planning and operating program. The full explanation is as follows:

F. Financial review
O. Operating plan

C. Control reporting

U. Understanding (interpreting results)

S. Strategic review

Financial review requires an innovative approach to business analysis. The review may require a definition of product and an understanding of perceived customer values. The business operation must be summarized by the department, identifying specific "customer services" to be performed. Although essential, this may be difficult due to the administrative structure of many companies. Fixed and variable costs should be identified to effectively control the departments. Plans that consider incremental actions and specific results are essential to an effective F.O.C.U.S. review.

An *operating plan* must be developed, considering each department and its specific contribution to the corporation's product. It is important to understand that each department must have a definite purpose—that is, to contribute to the delivery of a product to the company's customers. The operating plan must have measurable checkpoints and deliverable objectives. Target investing is used as the basis for evaluating and selecting alternative investment opportunities.

Control over the plan is essential, and can be accomplished through documented plans and periodic well-defined reporting. Reports should be brief and provide a narrative discussing specific action plans required to achieve the company goals.

Understanding the periodic reports, interpreting the results, and implementing contingency plans required to accomplish the corporate goals is an essential segment of the F.O.C.U.S. effort.

Strategic review and plans generally result from a F.O.C.U.S. review. It is important to understand that although immediate savings may result from a F.O.C.U.S. review, it is not necessarily the goal of the review. The F.O.C.U.S. review should be completed annually, preferably before budget preparation. It is essential to understand that this is not an exact accounting exercise. Approximations and reasonable estimates must be used to properly execute the program.

FINANCIAL REVIEW

Product Definition

How can we possibly ask "What is our product?" For example, it may be obvious that the product is "an electrical component, 4 × 6 inches, wafer thin, and is packed in cellophane. . . ." To question such a product is absurd.

An electronic equipment company will be used as an example throughout this exercise. Highlights of the operation are:

Annual Sales	$20,000,000
Number of customers	1,400
Number of different products	400
Number of sales invoices	12,000

Through careful review of the business, the product will be redefined. The product is not necessarily a tangible component, but could be considered a composite of:

Design	Size
Packaging	Delivery service
Order entry	Customer service
Product availability	Technical assistance
Advertising	Billing and collection
Sales terms	Pricing

Close communication with the sales and marketing department will help determine which factors are critical in the definition of "product." Each of these "deliverables" has a different perceived value to customers. The best method to determine the "product" is to establish a product matrix. This can be done by identifying the significant variables. It is important to keep the analysis simple, so that business conclusions can be easily developed and supported. Priorities must be established, concentrating only on the most important features of the "product." It is important that a disciplined approach be used to effectively complete the analysis.

Several sources of data can be used to define the product: employee brainstorming, internal reporting, and market research. We will explore the "brainstorming" and internal reporting as the "least cost" alternative in this review. Market research, although expensive, may be the best selection if company resources are adequate. Regardless of the source of product definition, the F.O.C.U.S. analysis can be completed in the same manner.

"Brainstorming" is the result of discussion and interaction between management and its subordinates. Through open discussion, factors considered to be important to the customer should be listed. Reasonable grouping (e.g., by product type or distribution channel) should be assigned to all captions. Priority rating (from most important—A—to least important—C) can be developed through discussion to determine the most important variables to the customers. Important features are summarized in the priority rating in Exhibit 13.1, segregated by trade channel.

The letters A, B, and C in Table 13.1 indicate priority from the most

Exhibit 13.1
Marketing Program—Priority Rating

	Trade Channel								
	Retail					Professional			
Product Description	W	X	Y	Z		W	X	Y	Z
Market									
Design	A	A	C	C		B	B	A	A
Size	C	A	B	B		C	C	A	A
Packaging	A	A	A	C		A	C	C	B
Advertising	A	A	B	C		A	A	A	A
Free goods	A	B	A	A		B	B	C	C
Marketing/accounting									
Pricing	C	C	A	A		A	C	C	B
Sales terms	B	B	A	A		A	A	B	C
Billing/collection	C	A	A	A		A	A	A	B
Distribution									
Delivery service	B	B	C	A		A	B	B	C
Order entry	C	C	C	C		C	B	A	A
Product available	B	B	B	A		C	C	B	A
Technical support									
Warranty	C	C	C	C		B	B	A	A
Service	B	B	A	A		C	C	A	A

important to the least important features. The product matrix has been segregated into action groups so that activities can be assigned to specific departments or individuals. The organization must determine the priority of *each part* of the product matrix, define acceptable levels of performance, and develop periodic reporting to support effective control of the tasks. This is very important, since each department will be competing for limited resources.

Internal reporting (company accounting records) is essential to properly support the definitions being developed in the product matrix. Product trends, customer profiles, and seasonal buying trends may all be available in the company accounting records.

Credit files include much information about the customers served and their product needs. The following customer profile may be contained in the customer credit file:

Annual sales	Number of employees
Total assets	Annual earnings
Growth trends	Expected volumes (not only for the company's line, but also competitors')
Type of legal structure (partnership, corporation)	Areas of specialty

In addition to credit application information, company credit files may include a large selection of customer data such as:

Sales activity (rolling twelve months, seasonal patterns, type of product sales)

Ship to/bill to locations

Payment history

Key contacts (president, purchasing agents, clerical people, accountants)

This data should be analyzed to better understand customer needs and the company product.

Sales analysis could include sales by territory, sales by product line, and sales by class of trade. Product line and territory sales are generally available. However, other essential information may be in accounting records. Through a group brainstorming effort, all factors related to customer trends should be identified. The information may already be included in the accounting records. Exhibit 13.2 is an example of sales by customer distribution channel.

This analysis indicates that most sales are through the retail and professional segment. As a result, these segments may be targets for continuing analysis. Other sales analysis may segment the sales by region, customer type, or location. A time limit for the sales analysis should be established

Exhibit 13.2
Sales Analysis, Customer Type

(000's $)

Product	Retail	Wholesale	Professional	Total
Prod W	500	1,000	200	1,700
Prod X	50	50	0	100
Prod Y	1,000	750	1,000	2,750
Prod Z	7,500	850	7,100	15,450
Total	9,050	2,650	8,300	20,000

and adhered to. If significant additional analysis is considered appropriate, it should be scheduled for a second iteration. Definition of the final components of the complete product at this time may be premature, but a "best guess" should be proffered.

The final step in product definition is to establish a "deliverable." A deliverable will be a standard unit to measure product performance. In Exhibit 13.3, although we may consider products W, X, Y, and Z as separate products, final analysis may reduce them to a larger product, an "electrical component."

Proper definition of product deliverable is essential, since this will serve as the basis for cost analysis. Ancillary products are not the essential products, or the largest profit makers, but instead support the primary or "deliverable" product.

Cost analysis is not intended to be an exact analysis, precise to the nearest dollar. Too often such analyses become mired in minutiae, lose focus on the analytical task to be completed, and never result in a proper conclusion. Cost analysis should provide a basis for evaluating the "costs of delivering" the product. A specific work program for developing the proper cost analysis is included in Exhibit 13.4. Although the lowest level detail in the trial balance is the basis of evaluation, judgment is required to properly complete the analysis. Estimates will be used to develop business conclusions. Due to this iterative approach, it is not unusual to establish several "product definitions" before the task force is comfortable with the final definition. Cost analysis will eventually result in a summary of fixed/variable costs and action items.

Exhibit 13.3
Electrical Component

S O R T E D

Description	Unit	Avg Price	Total
Chip - Micro circ A	3,655	17.55	64,145.25
Clip - 30 mm	46,423	1.37	63,599.51
Clip - 70 mm	7,554	2.99	22,586.46
Chip - Micro circ F	3,467	4.95	17,161.65
Chip - Micro circ I	2,455	6.45	15,834.75
Clip - 90 mm	366	35.07	12,835.62
Chip - Micro circ C	4,563	2.77	12,639.51
Clip - 80 mm	2,456	4.88	11,985.28
Clip - 10 mm	3,777	0.99	3,739.23
Chip - Micro circ P	23	137.99	3,173.77
Chip - Micro circ E	776	3.00	2,328.00
Clip - 20 mm	4,588	0.46	2,110.48
Chip - Micro circ J	256	7.44	1,904.64
Chip - Micro circ N	322	3.86	1,242.92
Chip - Micro circ K	33	27.99	923.67
Chip - Micro circ M	455	1.95	887.25
Clip - 50 mm	564	0.99	558.36
Chip - Micro circ L	47	3.97	186.59
Chip - Micro circ D	34	3.99	135.66
Clip - 40 mm	244	0.54	131.76
Chip - Micro circ H	13	9.23	119.99
Clip - 60 mm	23	3.97	91.31
Chip - Micro circ G	22	3.86	84.92
Chip - Micro circ B	233	0.19	44.27
Chip - Micro circ O	3	2.96	8.88

Costs are analyzed using three types of analysis: (1) total cost, or added value concept; (2) perceived value versus actual cost; and (3) fixed/variable allocations. A brief discussion of each of these analyses follows.

Total costs will be summarized and analyzed using the "added value" concept. This can be seen in the previous priority rating example. Total cost must be analyzed on a departmental basis so that "added value" can be understood. Added value is simply cost per unit of deliverable with an analysis of its value. In effect, this combines the perceived value and added value concepts in a single analysis. Exhibit 13.5 illustrates this concept. In this example, the customer perceived value is the $83.70 or

Exhibit 13.4
F.O.C.U.S. Work Program

                                                              Estimated
I. Financial Review

A) Review 1986, and 1987 chart of accounts;   6
define major service categories, by account number and
description

B) Prepare workpaper headings with a minimum   6
of the following detail
     -description
     -1986 Actual
       -Fixed
       -Variable
       -Total Expense
       -% to Sales
       -Average cost/ sales unit

     -1987 period to date actual
       -Fixed
       -Variable
       -Total Expense
       -% to Sales
       -Average cost/ sales unit

     -1987 Forecast - total year
       -Fixed
       -Variable
       -Total Expense
       -% to Sales
       -Average cost/ sales unit

C. Insert total expense for actual 1986, and   6
    year to date 1987

D. Identify fixed and variable expense components   12

E. Calculate all required ratios   4

F. Review all statistics; prepare
    a highlights report for review with the G.M.   32
    and Area Management.

Exhibit 13.4 (continued)

II Operating Plan

A. Review of financial highlights   2

B. Brainstorming of alternatives for variable   16
expenses and Selling Price tradeoffs

C. Isolate viable alternatives; brief discussion   8

D. Financial review of alternatives   8

E. Develop a plan with assigned responsibilities   8
and periodic progress checkpoints.

III. Control of Plan

Develop control reports which highlight results   8
of the plan

IV. Understand and Interpret the Results

A. Implement monthly control reports   4

B. Prepare highlights, and summary narrative of results   4

C. Participate in a monthly management review   4
of highlights.

V. Seasonal Review

Return to Step I (C)

Exhibit 13.5
Total Cost Summary

(000's $)

Description	Company Cost		Perceived Value
	Amount	%	
Product			
Cost	50.00	60	0.00
Duties	10.00	12	0.00
Freight	.50	1	0.00
Direct Selling			
Salary	6.00	7	0.00
Travel	.50	1	0.00
Promotional	4.00	5	0.00
Distribution			
Order entry	1.00	1	0.00
Packaging	.25	-	0.00
Profit	11.45	13	0.00
Total Sales	83.70	100	83.70

the purchase price. If changes are made to the "product," the perceived value by the customer may vary. The company costs represent total period costs (e.g., one year) divided by the number of "deliverables" sold to the customer. Note that the cost of delivering each type of service is summarized by product matrix component. This is an important concept, since reallocation of those resources may result in improved "perceived value." The reallocation of resources is a primary consideration in the operating plan development.

Perceived value is a concept that must be understood by the task force. That is, the customer will value certain parts of the product mix more than others. While the "perceived" value may be difficult to define quantitatively, *it is important to estimate the value* to ensure that the overall value of the deliverable is properly defined. An example of perceived value is co-operative advertising. Co-operative advertising is a joint venture between the volume seller and the manufacturer. Co-op advertising spreads the cost of creative development and production of advertising material among many beneficiaries. A complete 2-page advertisement for product Z may require 150 hours of creative advertising effort. The cost may total $15,000 and be excessive for a small retail outlet. As a "large" company, a manufacturer may fund a complete professional layout, reducing duplicate creative investment to achieve the same results. This is considered operating leverage. Exhibit 13.6 provides a brief analysis comparing the real cost and the perceived value of the co-op program. If the manufacturer were to charge $5,000 for the value of the layout, the customer total cost would be $30,000 (the sum of the media

Exhibit 13.6
Cost Analysis: Perceived Value

Description	Cost	Perceived Value
Advertising		
Development	$15,000	$15,000
Production	8,000	8,000
Media		25,000
Total	$23,000	$48,000
	=============	=============

cost [$25,000] plus the co-op fee of $5000). Assuming that 4 customers took advantage of the program, the value of the operating leverage in this case is the extended value of benefit (4 customers at $48,000 each), $192,000 with an investment of only $123,000. The operating leverage results from the reduced duplicated creative effort of $69,000 (3 customers at $23,000 each). Perceived value analysis is based solely on judgment, and is not an accounting exercise. Perceived values should be reviewed in a brainstorming session to create alternative spending plans.

Fixed and variable expenses should be thoroughly understood on a company or department basis. Some of the analysis may already have been covered in the baseline forecasting segment of this book. We will now concentrate on changes in variable expense and their effect on the marketing or product mix. A departmental trial balance could serve as the basis for this cost analysis. The analysis should be reviewed to identify decision variables that relate directly to product. Variable costs are incremental costs that change the product offering. Fixed costs are minimum costs to deliver the basic product. These definitions differ from those discussed elsewhere in the book, but management must adapt their thinking to that required in the prevailing situation. Criteria for determining "fixed" and "variable" expenses are as follows:

Fixed:
Existing commitments, such as leases, insurance contracts, or statutory requirements

Current base of operations (existing administrative force, sales force)

Required support related to previously defined fixed expense (e.g., fringe benefits of existing sales or administrative forces)

Variable:
Discretionary spending that can be shifted to other areas based on management decision

Additions to fixed expense should be considered variable expense in the period added

The key to the analysis is that *variable* costs relate to product mix changes.

In our example, "electronics business," all products must be shipped to the customers. A fixed/variable cost analysis may separate the basic service cost (mail of merchandise) from premium service (courier service). Measurable results of customer satisfaction may be quantified through changes in sales units, or dollars. The decision to increase variable costs should be a cooperative decision among the operating departments, since added variable costs in this "component of product" may reduce available spending in the other areas.

Delivery service in the above product mix may be an *A* priority for product *Z* in the retail segment and for product *W* in the professional segment. Note that the wholesale segment is indifferent as far as delivery service is considered. A comparative projection should be prepared identifying the cost and probable returns of the changes in variable spending. A simple example will illustrate (see Exhibit 13.7).

Note that increased sales volume results from the improved delivery service—air courier. Similar sensitivity analyses should be prepared for key components of the product mix offered. This example illustrates the potential impact of a change in a single variable—the type of delivery service. Through the use of a premium service, profits are projected to increase by 13 percent. Note that the analysis also provides for several management checks: time for expected performance; deliverable or increased units sold; base level expense; and specific variable spending targets. Reporting should also focus on these characteristics.

OPERATING PLAN

The formal analysis and most important portion of the F.O.C.U.S. program has been completed, and selected variable spending alternatives have been identified. The operating plan will result in prioritized opportunities and a final selection of variable expenses. The operating plan is simply a selection from the business alternatives developed in the formal review. It is necessary to evaluate the opportunities available and to prioritize them based on anticipated results. Contingency plans may also be developed to ensure that expected results are achieved.

The operating plan should include specific management actions and expected costs. These specific action plans will serve as the basis for determining the success of the program or the need for selection of contingency plans.

CONTROL

Control of the plan can be achieved through targeted reporting. This is reporting that identifies significant variances from the plan. Reporting should be clear, concise, and easily interpreted. Control reports should contain the necessary information to make a decision and to ensure that the overall plan is on target. Reports can take the shape of columns of numbers, highlighted variance reports, or perhaps graphic presentations. The reports should be frequent enough so that appropriate management actions can be implemented to alter the business operation.

Reports should also be targeted to report on the variables that can be changed to achieve the results required. For example, reports of sales dollar activity will not help in the management of an order entry

Exhibit 13.7
Comparative Analysis: Discretionary Spending

(000's U.S. $)

Activity	Sales	Gross Profit	Expenses	Contribution
Base Case	700	350	200	150
Alternate A				
Add premium shipping				
- sales increase	35	18		18
- 1st class increment cost			15	-15
Total impact	735	368	215	153
Alternate B				
Add premium shipping				
-Sales increase	90	45		45
- Overnight Air premium			24	-24
Total	790	395	200	171

function. Reports highlighting such factors as numbers of orders, average dollar value of order, number of minutes required to serve the customer, and so on would be useful for the customer service department. Other examples of reports which provide meaningful information include:

Department	Service
Shipping	Number of shipments
	Mail
	Air
	Rail
	Backorders
Order entry	Number of orders
	Mail
	Phone
	Average value per order
	Average time for service
Accounts payable	Value of discounts taken
	Number of checks processed
	Average time for processing

The objective of the above example is to report on a measurable service performed. Each service must relate to performance of a service for the customer.

UNDERSTANDING

Understanding the results of implementing the program and strategic review are traditional management activities. Understanding the results requires: measurement of specific targets or goals defined in the plan; pre-defined reports and reporting frequency; and follow-up review for any major variances from planned activities. The overall reports must high-light the company objectives, as well as department performance, of the variable management activities. In addition to these reports, overall department activity (e.g., the fixed portion of department activity) should be monitored. Exhibit 13.8 is an example of complete reporting.

Note that both department deliverables and overall spending are being measured in the report. It is important to understand that a page of numbers will not necessarily provide all the information required to properly interpret the department's performance. A brief narrative should cover any major activities and expected changes from plan. The narrative should also provide a brief explanation of variances. These explanations should not just be a repetition of the numbers, but actual business reasons for variance.

Exhibit 13.8
Expense Summary

Description	1987 Month	Fav (unf) to Budget		Prior year	
		Amount	Percent	Amount	Percent
Media					
Television	900	33	3.8%	-64	-6.6%
Radio	275	21	8.3%	-25	-8.3%
Newspapers	133	-12	-8.3%	-33	-19.9%
Magazine	275	21	8.3%	44	19.0%
Development					
Art	75	1	1.4%	-12	-13.8%
Layout	35	3	9.4%	-3	-7.9%
Consultant	79	-41	-34.2%	-39	-33.1%
Salaries	77	2	2.7%	-4	-4.9%
Fringe Benefits	18	1	5.9%	-2	-10.0%
Total	1867	29	1.6%	-138	-6.9%

```
Program comments:
-------------------------
```

a. Consultants required to bring development work on schedule.
Remember, that the staff was assigned to a priority project in April.
Program developed for timely feature on the TV tournament.

b. Major shift of print campaign from last year resulted in
higher incremental expenses. Daily papers contributing to sales
sales increase in Southern region as expected - +23%.

c. A major part of the Art commitment is being devoted to the 1988
ad program. Overall project on schedule. Review target - July...

STRATEGIC REVIEW

Strategic review should occur at least annually. The review should concentrate on a "macro" review of company performance. Trends rather than separate period performance should be the objective of the review. This can be completed best through graphs, comparing actual performance to planned performance (see Exhibit 13.9).

In additon, ratios should be measured to ensure performance targets

Exhibit 13.9
Graphic Analysis

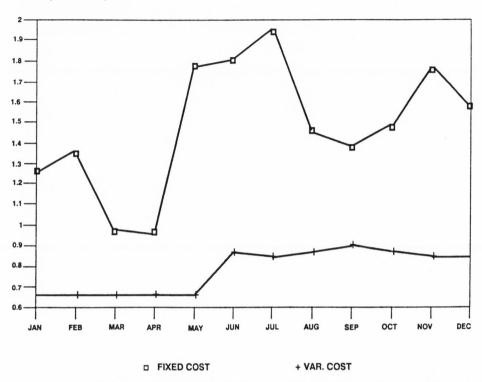

□ FIXED COST   + VAR. COST

make sense in relation to the overall company objectives. Items which could be measured include: units of deliverable sold; average cost per unit (e.g., fixed cost by department); and average cost per unit (e.g., variable cost by department).

Charts should be prepared using various mathematical averages to avoid distortion for a month's aberration. The strategic review provides a time for the company to revise the F.O.C.U.S. process. As noted above, the process should be completed on the macro level. Overall ratios developed in the prior year's review should be analyzed to determine if objectives were met. The review should also analyze the product definition to determine that the market has not changed dramatically.

SUMMARY

The F.O.C.U.S. review should be a window to examine the business operation. It is designed to be a compact analysis tool that will develop conclusions and specific operating plans. Due to its short timetable to implement—three to four weeks—it is an opportunity that should not be missed. If the full review is not completed, partial completion will provide additional understanding of your operation. Implementation of a F.O.C.U.S. review will provide:

Financial review which can be used in the budgeting or strategic planning process, as well as a more thorough understanding of the company product.

Operating plans based on incremental spending and specific measurable deliverables.

Control of specific plans through well-defined programs and reporting.

Understanding the results, since many of the company's objectives have been better defined.

Strategic review on a periodic basis with well-defined bases for measurement, since specific plans have been developed.

INDEX

About the Author

MICHAEL GENDRON is Vice President and Controller in the Optical Systems Division of Bausch and Lomb Inc. During his ten years with the company, he has been heavily involved in the international planning, acquisition, and management of offshore operations, as well as having divisional responsibilities for the United Kingdom, Hong Kong, China, Canada, and Middle East distribution areas.